In Adam's Garden

A Study of John Clare's
Pre-Asylum Poetry

Janet M. Todd

University of Florida Press
Gainesville · 1973

EDITORIAL COMMITTEE

Humanities Monographs

T. WALTER HERBERT, *Chairman*
Professor of English

J. WAYNE CONNER
Professor of Romance Languages and Literatures

RICHARD H. HIERS
Professor of Religion

G. PAUL MOORE
Professor of Speech

CHARLES W. MORRIS
Professor Emeritus of Philosophy

REID POOLE
Professor of Music

C. A. ROBERTSON
Professor Emeritus of English

MELVIN E. VALK
Associate Professor of Germanic Languages

Library of Congress Cataloging in Publication Data

Todd, Janet M.   1942–
  In Adam's garden.

  (University of Florida humanities monograph no. 39)
  Includes bibliographical references.
  1. Clare, John, 1793–1864. I. Title.
II. Series: Florida. University, Gainesville.
University of Florida monographs. Humanities, no. 39.
PR4453.C6Z954   821'.7   73–5897
ISBN 0–8130–0387–3

COPYRIGHT © 1973 BY THE STATE OF FLORIDA
BOARD OF TRUSTEES OF THE INTERNAL IMPROVEMENT TRUST FUND

PRINTED BY THE STORTER PRINTING COMPANY
GAINESVILLE, FLORIDA

Acknowledgments

I wish to thank both Professor Alton C. Morris, who proposed and greatly encouraged my study of Clare, and Professor Melvyn New, who improved it very much with his criticism and suggestions.

Thanks must go also to the Graduate School of the University of Florida for making possible the publication of this monograph.

For Aaron, Julian, and Clara

Contents

1. The Central Image   1
2. The Golden Age of Society   4
3. Eden as Nature   28
4. The Loss of Eden   53
5. The Creative Eden   81

1
The Central Image

THE MOST striking feature of John Clare's poetry is the inattention it has received from a century and a half of English readers. The seeds of this lack of interest may have been sown when John Taylor, Clare's first publisher, decided to present his poet to the populace as a Northamptonshire Peasant. In doing this he was exploiting a vogue for plebeian poetry, one which had carried to fame, among others, Stephen Duck, the poetical thresher, Mary Collier, the poetical washerwoman, and Henry Jones, the poetical bricklayer. Unfortunately, Taylor appears to have caught the tail end of this fashion with his poet: after the fascination with Clare's hobnailed boots had subsided, the vogue for his poetry was almost over.

A further reason for the lack of readership of Clare's work has been its scant publication. Even now there exists no complete text of his poems, and during his lifetime he was judged mainly on his first two volumes, *Poems Descriptive of Rural Life and Scenery*[1] and *The Village Minstrel and Other Poems*,[2] both of which contain formative rather than distinctive work. The asylum poems of his final period were, of course, unknown to his contemporaries.

In this century there has been a revival of interest in Clare's work, and several selected editions of his poems have been published. *The Poems of John Clare*,[3] edited by J. W. Tibble in 1935, remains the fullest of these, although a complete text is presently projected. The earlier selections tend to follow Taylor's emendations or, at least, his habit of emending, so they often present the

1. Ed. John Taylor (London: Taylor and Hessey, 1820).
2. (London: Taylor and Hessey, 1821).
3. (London: Dent, 1935), hereafter cited in text by volume and page.

poems much changed in grammar, spelling, and punctuation. The most recent texts, however, especially those edited by Eric Robinson and Geoffrey Summerfield,[4] try to follow Clare's manuscripts, thus presenting as far as possible the original poetry.

In this study I have treated Clare's pre-asylum verse, written prior to 1837. I have tried to establish the continuity of its themes and to suggest, in opposition to Harold Bloom's assertion of the poetry's dependence on Wordsworth, the essential distinction of Clare's mode from the dominant Romantic mode of the early nineteenth century.[5] In order to demonstrate the continuity and distinction in Clare's pre-asylum work, I have followed one particular theme that is dominant in the poetry and one whose treatment best records Clare's developing ideas and poetic techniques. Yeats thought every artist had a central symbol or image which could give a pattern to his entire work. The eulogistic images of the golden age for society and of Eden for nature are central to Clare's poetic development, and the attainment and loss of the ideal they represent is the progress chronicled by Clare's pre-asylum verse. The pattern is on the whole chronological, each phase being Clare's response to his personal situation and to the times in which he lived. Its treatment, therefore, requires some biographical details; for these I am primarily indebted to J. W. and Anne Tibble's *John Clare: His Life and Poetry*.[6] The elements of the pattern are not discrete, but each is a dominant theme at one particular time. The enclosure movement, for example, which Clare regarded as the primary instrument of the fall, is treated early in his verse when he is still describing the predominantly golden age of his society. It becomes, however, an intensely felt and realized subject when Clare understands fully the meaning of the nature which enclosure is destroying and the resulting human deprivation. Tracing this theme, I hope to suggest that, in the con-

---

4. *The Shepherd's Calendar* (London: Oxford University Press, 1964), hereafter cited as *SC*; *The Later Poems of John Clare* (Manchester: Manchester University Press, 1964); *Clare: Selected Poems and Prose* (London: Oxford University Press, 1966). A later edition of this last text, *Selected Poems and Prose of John Clare* (1967), has additional poems; hereafter cited as *SP*.
5. *The Visionary Company* (New York: Doubleday, 1961), p. 434.
6. (London: Heinemann, 1956), hereafter cited as *Life*.

sistency and development of his poetic response to his world and in the distinctive mode he uses to convey it, Clare is more than the peasant–poet initially presented to the nineteenth-century public and greater than the Wordsworthian shadow presented to our own.

2
The Golden Age of Society

IN 1821 John Clare set about writing his autobiography. The little that remains of his sporadic attempts was printed in 1931 in *Sketches in the Life of John Clare Written by Himself*.[1] He states there that he was born in 1793 "at Helpstone, a gloomy village in Northamptonshire, on the brink of the Lincolnshire fens" (p. 45). He was the only surviving son of Parker Clare, an illiterate flail-thresher, who yet managed to provide a little schooling each year for his son until the boy was eleven or twelve years old. Even before that time, however, Clare had had a taste of the severity of life: "In cases of extreme poverty, my father took me to labour with him, and made me a light flail for threshing, learning me betimes the hardship which Adam and Eve inflicted on their children by their inexperienced misdeeds, incurring the perpetual curse from God of labouring for a livelihood, which the teeming earth is said to have produced of itself before" (pp. 47–48).

The sad facts of Clare's later life are well known, better in fact than his poetry. John Taylor, Clare's publisher, in his introduction to the first volume of verses, sees the poet created in spite of his life, and he stresses the extraordinary nature of Clare's circumstances. Remarking that many poets have sketched poverty, he continues: "CLARE has here an unhappy advantage over other poets. The most miserable of them were not always wretched. Penury and disease were not constantly at their heels, nor was pauperism their only prospect. But he has no other. . . ."[2] Clare escaped from pauperism into the lunatic asylum in 1837, but in

1. Ed. E. Blunden (London: Cobden Sanderson, 1931).
2. *Poems Descriptive*, p. iii.

all else this comment, written in 1820 at the beginning of his poetic career, is remarkably prophetic.

Against the ever increasing poverty and bleakness of his life in the first half of the 1820s, Clare set the ideal of an earlier society, one which he felt he had known as a child and, as an adult, was seeing in its decline. This society had a harmony of elements, a sufficiency of means, and an essential equality of persons, all qualities that were slowly disappearing from his contemporary village. The society lived in harmony with external nature, neither plundering it nor completely controlling it, and it followed in its work and play the elemental fluctuations of time and season. In Clare's early poetry, this ideal, still partially realized by the society of his early maturity, is often referred to as golden.

But it was not alone a memory and present perception of his community that influenced Clare's formulation of a golden age. Taylor described thus the most important literary influence on Clare as a poet: "He was thirteen years of age when another boy shewed him Thomson's Seasons. . . . It called forth all the passion of his soul for poetry."[3] It was in the tradition of Thomsonian descriptive poetry that Clare began to write seriously, and he was clearly influenced by the conception of the golden age he found in Thomson and in the other eighteenth-century poets whom he subsequently read.

To understand Clare's golden age and its distinction from the social ideals of his Romantic contemporaries, it is necessary to appreciate his anomalous poetic position in 1821. One might begin by looking at the methods used by poets prior to Clare in treating rural subjects. In this regard, Joseph Addison in his essay on Virgil's *Georgics* has made a useful distinction between the georgic and the pastoral.[4] Both derive ultimately from Virgil, who wrote

---

3. Ibid., p. v. Raynor Unwin describes the immense influence of Thomson's poem on other descriptive poets, especially the peasant poets Stephen Duck and Robert Bloomfield: *The Rural Muse: Studies in the Peasant Poetry of England* (London: Allen and Unwin, 1954).

4. "An Essay on Virgil's Georgics," *Miscellaneous Works*, ed. A. C. Guthkelch (London: Bell, 1914), 2:4. Thomas G. Rosenmeyer makes a similar if not identical distinction between Hesiodic and pastoral poetry. He states that the *Georgics* are almost entirely Hesiodic, whereas the Eclogues are non-

two kinds of poems on rural themes. The first, the *Georgics,* which can be considered as one long work, was a didactic poem on the cultivation of the soil and the rearing of cattle and bees, interspersed with episodes, sketches of occupations, country recreation, and countrymen, and reflections on the dignity of labor, on the harmony of nature, and on patriotism. This epic-proportioned poem, according to Dwight L. Durling, gave rise in the eighteenth century to several distinct shorter genres.[5] One, the descriptive manual of husbandry, was practiced, for example, by John Philips and John Dyer. Others, such as the topographical poem, the character poem, and the reflective humanitarian poem, had a variety of exponents. Above all, the *Georgics* begot the descriptive and didactic poem, the genre that includes Thomson's *Seasons.*[6] The great popularity of Thomson's poem was perhaps a result of the increasing interest in natural history as the century progressed. This interest and Thomson's popularity gave an impetus, after *The Seasons,* to the writing of minute descriptions of nature, a characteristic of the georgic form. A second characteristic, associated by Durling with the tendency toward detailed accounts, is the realism the genre allows in the presentation of rural life, and a third characteristic of some genres descended from the *Georgics,* including the descriptive poem, is their postulation of a historical golden age. Virgil in his poem had described a golden age; this was both a convention and an actual time in the past and in the immediate future that contrasted with the strife-torn present. Thus it was both an ideal and an actuality. Following Virgil, several later georgic writers used the golden age both as a standard with which to judge the present and as an object of nostalgia, although they rarely suggested a future age of bliss. Two apparent exceptions to this generalization are George Crabbe and William Cowper. Both seemingly dismiss the golden age, but in fact the dismissal

---

Hesiodic: *The Green Cabinet: Theocritus and the European Pastoral Lyric* (Berkeley and Los Angeles: University of California Press, 1969), pp. 21, 24.

5. *Georgic Tradition in English Poetry* (New York: Columbia University Press, 1935), p. 60.

6. In *The Unfolding of the Seasons* (Baltimore: Johns Hopkins Press, 1970), Ralph Cohen argues that *The Seasons* is "a religious didactic poem" with a "unifying vision" (p. 3). This argument need not preclude its descriptiveness.

is of the pastoral age, which they felt to be a false idealization, and not of the georgic nostalgic one. In "The Village" Crabbe calls the pastoral golden age a "flattering dream" too long prolonged by poets ignorant of rural misery; Cowper is similarly critical, while at the same time he looks back fondly and recalls an Eden of biblical times.

The second genre has as its progenitor Virgil's *Eclogues* or *Bucolics*, written as imitations of the pastorals of Theocritus. In these the landscape and the golden age which is the subject are idealized, and in fact J. E. Congleton has said that Virgil set the pastoral on its long road to artificiality.[7] Yet, if he did, he ensured too that there would be some threat to the pastoral world described or some modification of it. In the first eclogue, for example, a dialogue of two shepherds, one still in his idyllic setting and the other dispossessed of his land by the government, the suffering of one shepherd is a qualification of the bliss of the other. Usually, however, the literary sophistication of the genre itself affects its subject. Indeed, from Puttenham to Empson, writers have stressed that pastoral poetry is sophisticated, the product of an urban and urbane culture. Its essence is not the countryside but the tension between the country setting and the sophisticated city life in which it is conceived and from which the rustics are viewed. For the writer in the Virgilian pastoral mode, the literature and the culture of the city are a necessity, and the swains he writes about are not those a contemporary countryman would have known but inhabitants of Arcadia, or at least of the poet's native land viewed as Arcadia from the culture and comfort of the city.

Throughout the long history of pastoral criticism, there had been a dispute concerning the content of the pastoral. The two sides crystalized in the eighteenth century into a Neoclassical School and a Rationalist School. Members of the former saw the aim of pastoral poetry as giving men an esteem for the virtues of a former classical age, and felt that the temporal setting should thus be the Virgilian golden age, an idealized time of plenty, prosperity, innocence, and simplicity. Unlike the georgic, the pastoral golden

7. *Theories of Pastoral Poetry in England, 1684–1798* (Gainesville: University of Florida Press, 1952), p. 5.

age tended to be timeless and, as Thomas G. Rosenmeyer has pointed out, "not concerned with history, or the sequence of evolutionary stages. Its time is here and now."[8] The poets of the Rationalist School wanted selected descriptions of English landscapes and English shepherds, as well as an abandonment of this convention of the golden age. In contradistinction to both schools, there arose the Romantic School, which had elements of the doctrines of each, as well as features peculiar to itself.[9] The Wartons, for example, although they wanted English subjects, did not reject the convention of the golden age of innocence and natural harmony as did the Rationalists, but they placed it in the English countryside rather than in the distant Arcadia of the Neoclassical writers. The Romantic poets followed the Wartons in this, and, in Congleton's words, the "chronological primitivism" of Virgil became the "cultural primitivism" of Wordsworth.[10] By the early nineteenth century, therefore, it was not unusual to see elements of the golden age in present rural life and to set in the English countryside the inhabitants of this mythical era. According to William Empson, in addition to this characteristic the Romantic pastoralists, as they may be termed, forwent the tension of pastoral poetry I have outlined. In its place they exhibited in their poetry a merging of poet and subject-matter as they transferred their own civilized dignity to their swains and heroes.[11] The result of this is less emphasis on the physical details of country life in Arcadia or Arcadian England and more on the poetical response and reflections of the new poet–hero.

Of the two traditions I have sketched, Clare's early verse evidences most the close descriptions of natural things and country

8. *The Green Cabinet*, p. 220.
9. The Neoclassical School may be exemplified in Pope, the Rationalist School in Ambrose Philips, and the Romantic School in Joseph and Thomas Warton. Congleton puts Wordsworth's "Michael" in the category of Romantic pastoral; Rosenmeyer, not judging it on the basis of eighteenth-century pastoral theory as Congleton has done, puts it outside the pastoral genre (p. 58). Yet it would be hard to consider "Michael" a georgic poem, for, unlike the eighteenth-century georgic poems, it is not predominantly descriptive. See Bloom, *The Visionary Company*, p. 178, for the symbolic implications of its natural details.
10. *Theories*, p. 116.
11. *English Pastoral Poetry* (New York: Norton, 1938), pp. 206–7.

people that Durling saw as characteristic of the georgic.[12] Although inevitably colored to some extent by the poet's emotions, these descriptions clearly exist for their own sake and not for any insight they might provide into the mental states of the poet. If Clare appears at all in the poem, it is as a perceiver and physical guide rather than as a feeling and imaginative creator.

By the time of Clare's second book of poems, in 1821, and more obviously by his third, in 1827, the georgic descriptive poem was clearly past its heyday. The new dominant mode of describing rural matters developed from the Romantic pastoral, a combination of idealized English country descriptions and the poet-swain's responses. This was the mode of Wordsworth, in whose poetry nature became the vehicle of emotions and the spiritual companion of isolated men rather than a harmonious background to a rural community. The descriptive poem over which the new genre had triumphed thus came to seem anachronistic to the reading public; yet Clare, in spite of growing evidence of its critical defeat, continued in this mode, a fact that helps to explain his sudden loss of public acclaim.

The change in taste from descriptive poetry to Romantic pastoral poetry was presumably gradual, but to Clare in the early 1820s it must have seemed to occur with remarkable speed. His first volumes of descriptive verse, in 1820 and 1821, were extremely well received, as had been the similar poetry of Robert Bloomfield, a poet whose social circumstances resembled Clare's. Within a few years, however, Bloomfield had died in poverty, and Clare's third volume of poems had failed hopelessly.

It is interesting to follow the poetic fates of Keats and Clare, who were both published by Taylor at about the same time. Keats' *Lamia, Isabella, The Eve of St. Agnes and Other Poems,* which came out in the same year as Clare's first book, was a failure beside Clare's initial success, but Keats' popularity grew tremendously in the years following while Clare's declined disastrously. In spite of high regard for each other, Keats and Clare seem to

---

12. Clare occasionally wrote poems that could be classed with pastorals from their form and subject matter, although the georgic realism of detail belies the classification. See "The Rivals" (I, 471).

have been aware that they were writing essentially different kinds of poetry. Of Keats, the new type of poet, Clare wrote, "He often described Nature as she appeared to his fancies, and not as he would have described her had he witnessed the things he describes." Clare was, furthermore, clearly doubtful about the "mystical" part of Romantic poetry, elements of which he found in Keats' work and later in Wordsworth's.[13]

Keats, on the other hand, was criticizing Clare from the new standpoint when he told Taylor that, in Clare's poetry, the "Description too much prevailed over the Sentiment."[14] This criticism is based on an essential tenet of Romantic poetry, but would hardly have been a fault in the older descriptive verse. A passage from Coleridge will serve to illustrate the new belief, although one could equally be taken from Wordsworth, Hazlitt, or De Quincey: "Images, however beautiful, though faithfully copied from nature, and as accurately represented in words, do not of themselves characterize the poet. They become proofs of original genius only as far as they are modified by a predominant passion . . . or lastly, when a human and intellectual life is transferred to them from the poet's own spirit. . . ."[15] Geoffrey Grigson, in his introduction to the *Selected Poems of John Clare* over a century later, echoes this idea when he asserts that "observation and description are not poetry," and that much of Clare's verse should therefore have been notebook jottings.[16]

Yet there is, besides the poetry of sentiment, a poetry of description, which makes the reader see almost by the naming of what is indeed there but was until then unnoticed. In his early poetry this is Clare's pre-eminent ability, as H. F. Cary noted in his letter to the poet: "What you most excel in is the description of such natural objects as you have yourself had the opportunity of observing, and which none before you have noticed, though every one instantly

13. *Sketches*, pp. 120–21; *The Prose of John Clare*, eds. J. W. and Anne Tibble (London: Routledge & Kegan Paul, 1951), p. 118.
14. Quoted in J. W. and Anne Tibble, *John Clare: A Life* (New York: Oxford University Press, 1932), p. 135.
15. *Biographia Literaria,* ed. J. Shawcross (London: Oxford University Press, 1907), 2:16.
16. *Selected Poems of John Clare* (Cambridge: Harvard University Press, 1950), p. 11.

recognises their truth."[17] Clare's descriptions of country people were equally as detailed as his natural descriptions, equally excellent, and equally disliked in 1827 by the reading public.

It is clear, then, that Clare in the early 1820s was writing in a genre that differed in its genesis and development from that adopted by most of his fashionable contemporaries. It is thus important to differentiate his golden age from that of the Romantic pastoralists like Wordsworth. Wordsworth's golden age country setting is derived from his belief that the most elemental passions are found most purely in the rustic situation, and it did not purport to be a realistic description of the externals of his society. However, since their subject was the social details themselves, the exponents of the descriptive poem tended to avoid idealization, aiming to present an actual picture of whatever society they knew. Clare's need for a model society, then, had to be served by the actual society he knew, although his use of his childhood and early adulthood provided the distance necessary to turn the real into an ideal. Clare's unique contribution to the georgic is that he located his ideal much closer in time to the moment of the poem than was usually the case. By doing so, he made the ideal as much a subject of his poetry as the world of reality which it was used to measure. But at the same time its temporal closeness to the present argues that Clare's ideal society at best is flawed; it is a perfection that yet must accommodate human imperfection.

"Helpstone,"[18] the first poem of Clare's first volume, *Poems Descriptive of Rural Life and Scenery*, provides an early example of the imperfection of the social ideal. The poem is a traditional topographical one, a description of a place with the narrator as both poet and perceiver within the poem. The narrator contemplates the town, and the prospect calls to his mind his vanished childhood in this setting. In lines that echo Gray's evocation of childhood in an earlier topographical poem, "Ode on a Distant Prospect of Eton College," the adjective "golden" is used to evoke the golden society of Clare's youth:

17. Quoted in *Life* (1932), p. 308.
18. Clare invariably spelled the name of his native village thus. Its modern spelling is "Helpston." I have followed Clare's usage when dealing with poems that include the name.

> And, oh! those years of infancy the scene,
> Those dear delights, where once they all have been,
> Those golden days, long vanish'd from the plain,
> Those sports, those pastimes, now belov'd in vain;
> When happy youth in pleasure's circle ran,
> Nor thought what pains awaited future man . . .
>   (I, 4).

The poem is a nostalgic lament for past joys and for a land that has been destroyed by enclosures; the poet sorrows for both "the vanish'd green" and his own time of greenness: "But now, alas! those scenes exist no more; / The pride of life with thee, like mine, is o'er." At the end the narrator relates his childhood and that of the land to a lost golden age in a combined apostrophe to Helpstone and his past: "Oh, happy Eden of those golden years / Which memory cherishes, and use endears." Here, then, it seems that Clare has already a conception of a golden age, and is locating it in the immediate past of his childhood. Yet, even thus distanced, the ideal is modified, and the modification reveals how ambivalent Clare's attitude is to the pre-enclosure village. Helpstone is described on the one hand as a paradise and on the other as "humble," "mean," "unletter'd," and a place of "useless ignorance." The final section of the poem with its undiluted nostalgia for "those charms of youth" and for "home" seems more an ignoring of the facts he has stated than a resolving of them.

"The Village Minstrel" is the title poem of Clare's second volume of verses. It is a long poem, written in Spenserian stanzas, a form perhaps suggested to Clare by Thomson's "Castle of Indolence" or James Beattie's "Minstrel." In many ways an unsatisfactory work in its discursiveness, sentimentality, and ambivalence, it yet presents most clearly the view of himself, his life, his art, and his society that Clare held in his earliest poetic years. Of this view, sentimentality and ambivalence are integral parts. Sentimentality conveys, through the self-indulgence that allows it, the horror that Clare felt at his lonely situation. It also excuses to some extent the passivity of the response he made at this time to the forces destroying his society. The ambivalence comes, as in "Helpstone," from the juxtaposition of idyllic and sordid aspects of rural society. Sometimes the latter are embedded in predominantly idyllic passages; sometimes they are isolated as the unique characteristics of a later age. This later, post-enclosure age is thus certainly unpleasant, but the pre-enclosure one is not entirely golden. Once again, then, the detailed description of the georgic mode, combined with the temporal closeness of the age he described, mitigated against Clare's presentation of a simple ideal for a complex reality.

In the first section of "The Village Minstrel," the village is a society that lives in harmony with nature; it has left the wild places relatively untouched for the poet Lubin to wander in, and it marks the progress of the seasons with traditional festivities. It is a place of social harmony among the different classes, where man and master drink together and where workers toil in social freedom in the open fields. It is a place too of innocent rural love. At the same time, however, the village is a center of rowdiness and gossip, of "parish-huts where want is shov'd to die," and of "harden'd brutes," whose insensitive cruelty destroys women as it later destroys nature, and whose fun is of a kind:

> Here 's 'Civil Will' too, with his 'pins and pegs,'
> And he makes glorious fun among the chaps:
> 'Boys, miss my pegs,' he cries, 'and hit my legs,
> 'My timbers well can stand your gentle taps,'
> Though sure enough he gets most ugly raps,
> For here the rustic thinks the sports abound;
> Whose aim at 'Civil's' legs his fellows caps
> Meets most applause—still 'poor Will' stands his ground,
> 'Boys, throw your copper salve, and make another wound.'
> (I, 149)

Thus, if the society is still golden, it is rather in the evening than in the morning of the golden age, and the simple nostalgic ideal Clare sometimes postulated in other poems is finally much qualified.[19]

19. See "The Harvest Morning" (*SP*, p. 7), "The Cottager" (*SP*, p. 30), and "The Cellar Door—A Ballad" (*SP*, p. 46).

Likewise, the presentation of Lubin, the narrator–poet and an image of Clare, is complex. In the initial stanza of the poem, he is a "humble rustic," humming "his lowly dreams," singing "what nature and what truth inspires." The other side of his situation is made clear in the second stanza where he is a "luckless clown," treated with "black neglect," whose fancy is worn down by "toil and slavery." A further modification of the picture of the rustic swain is effected by the third stanza, which describes his father as a "hind born to the flail and plough, / To thump the corn out and to till the earth." The vocabulary here reinforces the contrast with the initial stanza, for the plainness is far from the poetic diction, the "muse," "charms," and "pastures," of the opening of the poem.

In the second section of "The Village Minstrel," Clare describes the coming of enclosure. After this event, the picture presented of the pre-enclosure world loses much of its complexity, and the idyllic, natural, harmonious side of the older village is emphasized almost to the exclusion of the cruel and insensitive elements that Clare had recorded earlier and that had, in a way, allowed the enclosure movement to proceed. Sitting with the shepherds to bewail the loss of the past, the poet finds he can remember only the golden characteristics of the old village life, its festivities, its freedom, and its harmonious relationship with nature; it is these he laments when he

> Talk[s] o'er with them the rural feats of May—
> Who got the blossoms 'neath the morning dew
> That the last garland made, and where such blossoms grew ...
> (I, 157).

The effect of the social change on Lubin is similarly uncomplicating. Where his attitude had been ambivalent toward the society which he had at once revered and yet constantly escaped from into nature, after the coming of enclosure it is one of total sympathy with the dispossessed peasants. His alienation from the dominant men who have forced the enclosures on his village therefore needs no qualification. So, too, he finds himself at one with the land that has been despoiled, and he can take a simile for himself from the enclosed world. He is like a "cornflower" in a field of grain, the isolated natural being whose kind once covered the whole land before man-controlled grain was sown in usurpation. Lubin claims an identification with a society with which he was, before its destruction, only in partial accord, and he has given that society a natural rightness that it only partly possessed when it existed as a chronological actuality.

In Clare's first two volumes of poetry, the contrast between his descriptions of a golden age society and his portraits of that same society's faults is often echoed in the contrast between ornamental language and literary verse forms and his dialect words and conversational rhythms. In his introduction to *Poems Descriptive*, Taylor draws attention to Clare's peasant vocabulary, although as he edited the poems he tried to delete much of it, substituting in its place a diction he felt more suitable to the sort of verse Clare should have been writing. At first Clare himself seemed unsure of the suitability of his rustic diction for the traditional themes of poetry, and thus, in a very early poem like "Summer Evening," there is a distinct difference between the vocabulary used to describe the village characters he knew and that used to portray nature and postures traditionally poetic. He described his fellow rustics in this way:

> Now the hedger hides his bill
> And with his faggot climbs the hill
> Driver Giles wi rumbling joll
> And blind ball jostles home the roll (*SP*, p. 11).

At the end of the poem, however, he saw himself in a poetic, contemplative position, lying

> Thoughtful stretching on my bed
> Listning to the ushering charms
> That shakes the Elm trees mossy arms (*SP*, p. 14).

Later Clare became surer of his own rustic diction, and he could write to Taylor, who proposed changes in *Poems Descriptive*, that

"'Eggs on'" might be provincial "but it is common with the vulgar (I am of that class) & heartily desire no word of mine to be altered."[20]

In the poems that followed Clare's publication of his first volume of poetry, the contrast between the ideal and unpleasant aspects of village society was often made deliberately and effectively through juxtaposition, reinforced by a contrast between literary and colloquial diction. In "Rural Morning" (I, 204), for example, the idyllic aspects of the rural scene are juxtaposed to the brutish in the figures of the horseboy Hodge and the maiden. The former's gait is "soodling," while the girl is as "sweet as the thyme that blossoms where she kneels."

An even more effective, deliberate use of the contiguity of details is found in "Autumn" (I, 169). The harmonious picture of rural folk, rustic boys, cowboys, and scrambling shepherds, all in a setting of red-berried trees under "thin-spun clouds," is qualified by the presentation of the other side of rural society, the murdering gunner whose destructive act breaks this harmony, just as surely as winter destroys the pageant of autumn. In this poem, both the literary experience of the season, which is the contemplation by the poet of natural harmony, and the country folk's active experience of it are modified, the former by the cruelty of man, the latter by the cruelty of winter. Thus the poem presents a drama of winter overtaking summer:

> More coldly blows the autumn-breeze;
> Old winter grins a blast between;
> The north-winds rise and strip the trees,
> And desolation shuts the scene. (I, 174)

But there is another drama, that of a poet trying to create an image of a golden society into which the other cruel reality he knows intrudes:

---

20. Cited in *Life*, p. 65. Adverse criticisms of *The Village Minstrel* were frequently directed at Clare's use of provincialisms or vulgarisms. On receiving one of these criticisms, Clare commented, "That Poets should conform their thoughts or style to the taste of the country by which he means fashion is humbug" (*Life*, p. 83).

> But hide thee, muse, the woods among,
> Nor stain thy artless, rural rhymes;
> Go leave the murderer's wiles unsung,
> Nor mark the harden'd gunner's crimes.[21] (I, 173)

Most of the poems of Clare's early volumes deal with the pre-enclosure rustic society and himself within that society. Very rarely is the presentation simply of either an ideal society or a degenerate one. The contradictions and complexities of the world he portrays reflect Clare's attitude toward the society he had both revered and avoided as a child and youth, and reveal the difficulties inherent in the use of childhood as an ideal. As he studied more deeply his rustic neighbors, and considered the struggle and hardship of his own adulthood, the balance he had achieved and exploited, in such poems as "Autumn," between the golden and tarnished aspects of reality was gradually destroyed. The tension created by the disturbance of such a balance and the straining of the poet to re-establish it give to Clare's depictions of the twilight of pre-enclosure England an emotional and dramatic interest that is not usually characteristic of georgic descriptive poetry. These qualities are pre-eminently seen in *The Shepherd's Calendar,* where the use of a contemporary setting exacerbates the problem of the intrusion of unpleasant aspects of reality into the ideal.

In 1823, at Taylor's suggestion, Clare embarked on *The Shepherd's Calendar,* a descriptive poem of village life longer than anything he had yet written.[22] It was advertised in 1824 but not published until 1827. During the two years following, only four hundred copies were sold, and the reading public appears to have agreed with Taylor when he expressed his dislike of Clare's poetry "describing common things" and advised him to speak of the "Ap-

---

21. The influence of Thomson seems especially strong in "Autumn." The lines on winter are reminiscent of Thomson's "Winter," lines 1032–33, and the idea that hunting is no subject for the muse echoes line 379 of Thomson's "Autumn."
22. Robinson and Summerfield print only the descriptive poems in their volume of *The Shepherd's Calendar.* The 1827 volume consisted of descriptive poems, village stories designed to complement them, and other poems.

pearances of Nature each Month more philosophically . . . or with more Excitement."[23] Indeed, in "May" Clare shows himself, in a moment of self-distrust, aware of the possible public antipathy to his type of descriptive verse:

> My wild field catalogue of flowers
> Grows in my ryhmes as thick as showers
> Tedious and long as they may be
> To some, they never weary me (*SC*, p. 53).

Yet it is perhaps a measure of his need for an ideal and of his realization that the decline of his village was irrevocable that he undertook and completed, in spite of discouragement, a long descriptive record of society's pristine glory and decay.

The Shepherd's Calendar is organized by the seasons, month by month in the manner of many other poetic and prose "calendars."[24] It is not structured so that the parts form a complete whole or so that the whole would be damaged by the removal of any part, and, aside from its monthly framework, it has no clear or explicit thematic unity. What unity it has is that of the descriptive poem of the georgic tradition. Like *The Seasons*, it is made up of many differing elements, but the relationships among these various elements have much in common. What at first appears to be digressive in *The Seasons* is considered by John Chalker, for example, as integrated on a thematic level in a series of contrasts and contiguities, basic to georgic poetry since Virgil.[25] In the same manner, along with descriptions of workmen, animals, and trees, Clare wrote in his poem also of enclosure, the cruelty of the rich to the poor, and the loss of childhood. Each subject is separable or removable, but each gains meaning from its position in a larger whole and from the contrasts and comparisons into which it enters.

23. *SC*, p. viii. James Hessey criticized the poems of *The Shepherd's Calendar* because they abounded in "description" and lacked "sentiment and human interest" (quoted in *Life*, p. 118). The reviewer in the *Literary Gazette* thought the poetry not romantic enough (*Life*, p. 122).

24. This organization is prominent among Hesiodic poems, according to Rosenmeyer (p. 21).

25. *The English Georgic: A Study in the Development of a Form* (Baltimore: Johns Hopkins Press, 1969), p. 134.

One contrast basic to the georgic genre and occurring in the poems of Virgil and Thomson is that between the golden age and the iron age. Clare differs from his predecessors, when he uses this contrast, in being primarily concerned with the former. Again, although Clare sees his golden age as a historical time, as Virgil had before him, he is at odds with the Virgilian tradition in two respects.

The first is that, since his golden age is in his experience not at its height, there is some modification of the true golden age state when man was supplied by nature and so had no need of agriculture. In Virgil's first georgic, the first golden age is a time when "no peasant vexed the peaceful ground." For Clare, this pure golden age existed before Adam's fall, and, as it is described in the *Sketches,* it has the Virgilian lack of agriculture.[26] In the experienced golden age of Clare's youth and early manhood, however, man does plow for himself, and this work is joyful like the bees' work. Enforced toil for money characterizes the iron age, as does the excessive plowing of the land. A possible influence on this conception of a modified golden age is Salomon Gessner's *Death of Abel,* which Clare as a boy regarded highly. In this work, Adam recollects the true golden age before the fall, while Abel experiences the modified golden age of moderate labor, without want or tyranny. Cain, forced to labor against his will, experiences an iron age of cruelty and greed.[27]

The second difference between Clare's conception and the Virgilian tradition concerns Virgil's assertion that the golden age was destroyed so that man might by his labor recreate a paradise. Thus his harvest scene, a picture of labor and striving, is the central scene of the first georgic. In Clare's poem, too, the moderate labor and plenty of the golden age are in opposition to the industry and hardship of the iron age; but where Virgil and Thomson welcomed the new era, Clare sees it wholly as a deterioration. There is no fortunate fall in his mythology. His harvest scene in "August" is therefore very different from those of his predecessors.

26. P. Virgilius Maro, *The Georgics,* trans. John Dryden (1697; New York: The Heritage Press, 1953), p. 14; *Sketches,* p. 47.
27. *Death of Abel* (London: J. Dodsley, 1765), pp. 1–11, 14, 38–92.

His description starts with a picture of the village, empty because the people have gone to the fields; thus, although it is but late summer, the village has become like winter: "Doors are shut up as on a winters day." The comparison gains added significance from the traditional association of the golden age with spring and summer. In the fields the men are toiling, but their work does not elevate them; it is, on the contrary, degrading, for it is unnatural. There is an image of this unnaturalness in the little child "sun burnt and stooping with a weary hand," while "crackling stubbles wound its legs and feet." Happiness is imagined by the child as "ease," "an idle hour" to play with the insects that are "strangers to the moiling day." Because, then, labor is not natural to the other creatures, it is an imposition on man's freedom too, and the association of industry with cruelty further emphasizes this point. In the fields the laborers with their glittering sickles turn up the little animals that once lived in freedom there, and "spread an instant murder all around." Further, industry breeds not only cruelty but greed, and the month ends with the beggar boys hungry because none will give them food through "thrifts error," and because fear of savage punishment prevents them from thieving. This then is the social condition at the end of the description of laboring man; this is the fruit of his unnatural labor. It is clear that for Clare there is no compensation for lack of ease and free, moderate labor. By puncturing the myth of the joy of manual work, Clare is in the tradition of Stephen Duck, the thresher, who, like Clare, was acquainted with the labor he described and was equally emphatic about its joylessness.

The Shepherd's Calendar is, then, primarily a description of the qualified golden age of Clare's early maturity. He does not always differentiate the pre- and post-enclosure ages, but it seems that the time of the poem is Clare's present, in a partially enclosed society. Throughout the poem there are suggestions that the golden age is not at its height, effected primarily through the juxtaposition of idyllic scenes depicting the harmony of man with nature with those that clearly state his separation from it. The decadence is further implied in the poet's frequently expressed nostalgia for early childhood, seen as a better time than the present of the poem.

There is, however, within *The Shepherd's Calendar,* demonstrated by "August," a progression to something approaching the iron age, a progression that is not a linear development but a cumulative one. Each month has contrasting, juxtaposed aspects, but the later months have rather more of the iron age characteristics than the early ones.

Appropriate to a poem organized on the seasons and describing the iron age characteristics incrementally as the months pass, the new age is often associated with winter. Just as the year declines into winter from the harmony and joy of the spring months, in the same way the movement toward the iron age is a decline and can be expressed in terms of the annual fall into winter. In keeping with this parallel, the enclosure movement, the chief symbol for the new wintry age, has the same effect on nature as winter itself: in "November" a "dreary nakedness the field deforms," and in many enclosure poems, such as "The Mores," a similar nakedness and deformity result from the winter man brings. November's wintry bareness is then prophetic of the coming bareness from enclosure, a bareness which is not, however, a prelude to a new spring. The thematic pattern here follows the seasonal one, much as it does in *The Seasons,* where Thomson suggests a combined seasonal and social decadence from the golden age of spring as man loses his innocence and nature its freshness and beauty.

For the myth of the two ages, the central month is "June"; it is also the central section of the poem since "January" has two parts. After "June," although the same yoking of pure and corrupt aspects of society continues, the emphasis shifts decisively toward the latter. It is, therefore, an epitome of Clare's method of juxtaposition and the modification of aspects it causes, and of the iron age dissociation of man from nature and man from man.

"June" opens with a picture of nature active but idle; the unsubordinated insects are not busy toiling but instead are dancing and "reeling" in the sun, while flies and bees make melody for their frolics. All the creatures are bent on pleasure alone, and even the flowers are longing sensuously for the dew and the bees' honey to fill them. Everything is colorful, gay, and free, and the flowers have grown over and conquered "the weeders labour." The first hint of anything other than freedom, innocence, and merriment is the mention of the workmen; although they come merrily into the fields each morning, they soon become weary and long for rest. Meanwhile, like nature avenging itself on those who unnaturally work in summer, the gadflies drive the herdboy and his cows to run destructively into the corn that is the care of the toiling human beings: the herdboy, seeing his cows rushing into the corn,

> Is forcd his half made oaten pipes to drop
> And start and halloo thro the dancing heat
> To keep their gadding tumult from the wheat
> Who in their rage will dangers overlook
> And leap like hunters oer the pasture brook
> Brushing thro blossomd beans in maddening haste
> And 'stroying corn they scarce can stop to taste
> (SC, p. 64).

In the midst of their work, the laborers yearn for the coolness nature provides, and, when the plowman stops his work to drink, he is loath to leave the "swaily" brooks where the ring dove broods "oer its idle nest." In striking contrast to the bird's fitting inactivity, the plowman in this cool and pleasant place must "stand to breath and whipe his burning face." When the human toil starts up again, its lack of harmony with the world around is matched by the dissonance of the sounds it makes, the "shrill whistles barking dogs and chiding scold." The unnaturalness of the labor is paralleled by the unnatural imprisonment of the sheep who are shut out from the sun as if in winter. All that relieves the wintry hardness of the laborers' toil is ale-drinking, and even that is now but an echo of former jollity, "the thread bare custom of old farmers days." The true spirit of comradely festivity, and the songs and merriment that expressed it, existed only in "the good old times," "when leathern bottles held the beer nut brown / That wakd the sun wi songs and sung him down." But, at this point in his reminiscences, the old man, whose memory alone bears witness to the true rural age of gold, is interrupted in his tale by the need to toil again:

> Thus will the old man ancient ways bewail
> Till toiling sheers gain ground upon the tale
> And brakes it off (*SC*, p. 66).

By "June" the "old farmers days" have passed away, together with the "old freedom that was living then / When masters made them merry wi their men," and no social distinctions of dress and speech marred the village harmony. Nonetheless, a "time torn remnant" of the rural happiness remains. Girls still crown the swains with flowers after the shearing, and are, for the moment, flowers themselves; in Clare's poetry this is a frequent metaphor for the harmony of man and nature. But, from this time, the poet looks forward to a later age when even this expression of concord will be totally impossible, when the flowers the girls become will be as dead as the enclosed fields:

> As proud distinction makes a wider space
> Between the genteel and the vulgar race
> Then must they fade as pride oer custom showers
> Its blighting mildew on her feeble flowers (*SC*, p. 69).

After "June" the description of a golden age is continued in, for example, the picture of ripe country maidens set in ripening corn, but the contrast between man's enforced toil and nature's idle profusion and free labor is increasingly marked. So, too, the opposition is more and more obvious between man's unnatural, because unnecessary, cruelty and nature's beauty and helplessness. In "July," the swain, forced to work in the fields, feels no kindred spirit with the free bees laboring voluntarily at their honey: "He tears their small hives mossy ball / Where the brown labourers hurded all." Likewise, the separation foreshadowed at the end of "June" between the "genteel" and the "vulgar," between employer and laborer, becomes a fact of existence in the later months. In "November," the boy employed to scare the crows from the wheat envies the hunters riding by. For him "sullen labour hath its tethering tye," but they hunt freely and merrily. The only poor people then exempt from the unwilling toil are the gipsies, described in "October." But they too will have their freedom curtailed as nature itself becomes circumscribed, for they can camp only on land left unenclosed, "on commons where no farmers claims appear / Nor tyrant justice rides to interfere."

After the constant qualifications of village harmony and traditional jollity, it is not surprising that the description of the seasonal festivities in the final month, "December Christmas," should have a haunted quality. The impression here is of a poet holding onto a remnant of a passing way of life. To present the better age surrounded by manifestations of a worse, he must be selective in his details. Therefore, although the happy time is depicted minutely, there are hints that such happiness is not the whole picture. For example, the mirth of the season beguiles "care," and there are reflections embedded in the account of the passing of simple customs as pride grows. Soon these customs will live only in "the poet's song." A further modification of the mirth of the season is the consistent association of these traditional joys with childhood. They are therefore most intense for the adult in memory, not in their present condition. In addition, the absence of any mention of Christ in a section devoted to Christmas perhaps implies that this dark December will not be followed by the resurrection and rebirth of spring.

The various themes of *The Shepherd's Calendar*—the passing of the best age of rural England, the dissolving of the harmony between man and nature, the value and beauty of the older society as well as the incipient vulgarity and cruelty—are occasionally clearly expressed, but more often they are implicit in the imagery or in the contrasts of juxtaposed descriptions, and they are usually most powerful when least explicit. This poetic method is not the only or even the prevailing way of a poet like Wordsworth, and it is probable that much of the adverse criticism that *The Shepherd's Calendar* has received has come from judging it by standards inapplicable to its form and method.[28] Taylor's expressed dislike of Clare's unphilosophical descriptions and his emendations and dele-

28. See the assertions of "Tintern Abbey" and *The Prelude*, for example. Concerning a passage of *The Excursion*, Bloom comments, "This kind of poetry *has* a palpable design on us, and does not disguise it" (p. 168).

tions of this poem best represent the sort of misunderstanding that it has suffered; they also make clear that his bases for judgment are far from Clare's poetic purposes.

Many of the deletions of social criticism, like that at the end of "June" where Clare complains of the growing class distinctions, were possibly deemed offensive to prospective conservative patrons, but they served in the poem to qualify the picture of a romantic golden age society, which Taylor sometimes appears to consider Clare's sole theme, and suggested at the same time the growing rural decadence.[29] Similarly, "July," in which Clare depicts the complexity of the rural situation, its idyllic beauty and its vulgarity and cruelty, was totally rejected by Taylor in favor of a second version in which, although the laborers still wish occasionally for the ease of the insects' lives, the picture is much more "poetic" and pleasant and thus more unified in effect. The two descriptions of rural beauty, of a single maiden in the later version and of several in the earlier, can serve to illustrate this; in the second version, which Taylor approved, the girl is described with

> ... red lips never paled with sighs
> And flowing hair and laughing eyes
> That oer full many a heart prevailed
> And swelling bosom loosely veiled
> White as the love it harbours there
> Unsullied with the taints of care (*SC*, p. 135).

In the earlier rejected account, the girls have the same attributes:

---

29. For a discussion of Taylor's editing of *The Shepherd's Calendar*, see E. Robinson and G. Summerfield, "John Taylor's Editing of Clare's *The Shepherd's Calendar*," *Review of English Studies*, n.s. 14, no. 56 (November 1963):359–69. The authors conclude that Taylor's modifications and many of his omissions were made according to three criteria: that the subject matter was too "low," too sensual or physical; that the attitudes were too radical or discontented; that the language and syntax were provincial. Ian Jack finds the condensed account of this editing "unfair and misleading." See *Some British Romantics*, eds. James V. Logan, John E. Jordan, and Northrop Frye (Ohio State University Press, 1966). In *English Literature, 1815–1832* (Oxford: Clarendon Press, 1963), Jack writes of Taylor, "There is no doubt that he made improvements in the text of Clare—notably in ... *The Shepherd's Calendar*" (p. 30). Clare undoubtedly welcomed many of Taylor's suggestions and changes, and several were probably improvements; yet the criticisms of Robinson and Summerfield still appear substantially valid.

> Wi light dress shaping to the wind
> And trembling locks of curly hair
> And snow white bosoms nearly bare
> . . . .
> Like lingering blossoms of the may
> From clowns rude jokes they often turn
> And oft their cheeks wi blushes burn
> . . . .
> Some in the nooks about the ground
> Pile up the stacks swelld bellying round (*SC*, p. 71).

The adjectives reveal a difference of precision between the two versions. In the first the bosom is "nearly bare," in the second "loosly veiled"; in the later version the hair is "flowing," in the earlier "trembling," an adjective that suits the comparison with the "lingering blossoms of the may," which are the last to fall though tugged at by the wind. The whiteness is like "love" in the later version, like "blossoms" in the earlier, an image that reinforces the constant association in the poem of girls and flowers, both in their beauty and in their delicacy. In the early version, this delicacy is contrasted with the coarseness of the clowns, and is a prelude to the pain of women's lot, hinted at by the next detail, stacks like swollen bellies. As these are inevitable because of the progress of the months, so the girls' fates are somehow made to seem inevitable. In the later version, however, the village beauty is "unsullied with the taints of care," an ideal maiden in an ideal world, and the passage fails to reinforce the ambivalent picture of "golden" rural life Clare paints throughout *The Shepherd's Calendar.*

The Shepherd's Calendar is Clare's last long descriptive poem and his last sustained attempt to describe the pre-enclosure village society. After this, possibly because his own taste was moving with the times, possibly because his loneliness forced him to look into himself and to his nonhuman surroundings for stimulus, he turned increasingly for his subjects to nature and his own sensibility, the prevailing topics of the poetry in his age. *The Shepherd's Calendar* marks the end of a phase of Clare's poetic life. Yet, in spite of his progression from it and in spite of its unpopularity with post-Romantic readers, Clare's treatment of his society in his early poems does not represent an anachronistic dead end which he followed because of his isolation from Romantic theory and practice.[30] Clare wrote in a genre that has not retained its popularity, but one which has qualities of visual precision and factual truthfulness lacking in more subjective genres. Because of these qualities, Clare's early poems present collectively a picture of rural society which is nowhere attempted by the major Romantic poets and which is rare in all English literature.

The change in Clare's subject matter after *The Shepherd's Calendar* suggests that he became less concerned with society and with an ideal image of it. It also suggests that Clare had resolved the tension between his golden image and the increasingly unpleasant reality only by escaping from it. After 1824, the theme of the golden age is eclipsed in Clare's poetry. The disappearance supports the impression given by his letters that, as time went by, it was becoming harder for him to find any elements of his ideal society in his rural community, a community that by 1824 he knew would always imprison him in its cruelty and crudity.

30. Ian Jack considers the 1827 *Shepherd's Calendar* volume "by far the best of the poems that Clare published during his lifetime" (*Some British Romantics*, pp. 207–8). It certainly surpasses Clare's previous volumes, although it is, I believe, equaled by Clare's final volume, *The Rural Muse*.

3
Eden as Nature

BETWEEN 1824 and 1832, the period following his literary success, Clare became more and more isolated from the literate and urbane society that had for a short space of time adopted him and allowed his "hard-nailed shoes" to clatter on their "marble & boarded floors." Even at the height of his fame, however, Clare had been aware of the anomalous and precarious nature of his social intrusion, and the discomfort he felt during his interview at Burghley House was an odd mixture of humility and pride: "I had been about half an hour eying the door & now & then looking at my dirty shoes & wishing myself out of danger of soiling such grandeur." Of the intrusion of the leisured classes into his own world, he records several examples. Groups of the curious came to assure themselves that he was "the son of a thresher & a labouring rustic," and Clare's reaction to a typical visit was similar in its humility and pride to his reaction at Burghley House, but distinct in its bitterness: "On finding me a vulgar fellow that mimickd at no pretensions but spoke in the rough way of a thoroughbred clown they soon turnd to the door & dropping their heads in a goodmorning attitude they departed."[1]

In the mid-1820s, however, Clare's bitterness at his treatment seems to have increased with the apparent failure of his hopes for literary success; his feeling must have been augmented by the news that the poet Robert Bloomfield had died neglected and poor. Bloomfield was much admired by Clare, and the two were comparable in their evanescent fame. Clare wrote to his friend Inskip of the deep effect of this death on himself in a letter that summed up the life of a true poet as "Dissapointment and pov-

---
1. *Prose*, p. 69.

erty."[2] The journal Clare began writing in September 1824 charts the simultaneous progress of his alienation from his peers, no doubt the partial result of his worsening financial circumstances and of his increasing ill health. His fellows, it was becoming obvious to him, had neither innocence, nor freedom, nor harmony with nature, those qualities he had postulated for them in his golden age poems. Thus he could describe bitterly to Taylor his once rural paradise: "I live in a land overflowing with obscurity & vulgarity far away from taste & books & friends."[3]

But Clare's alienation from his society was not, strictly speaking, a new phenomenon. It had been incipient in his relationship with his fellows even when he was writing of them as rustics in a golden age, and the first seeds of the feeling that matured after 1824 are evident in several early autobiographical poems that deal with images of the poet. In "The Village Minstrel" (1821), Lubin is a poet who feels out of harmony with the society into which he has been born, but he is not sufficiently confident of his poetic identity to find compensatory pride in his difference from others. Thus his response is self-pity and sentimentality.[4]

In the poems that followed "The Village Minstrel," Clare tried to identify what it was that separated him from his neighbors who were born and raised as he was in the still golden world. At the same time, the gradual collapse of the old ideal of a social golden age forced him to formulate a new one. He found it in nature, and it was connected to his poetic gift, for it was nature that had fostered that gift. To express and investigate the new ideal of nature, Clare evolved a new sort of poetry to coexist with his descriptive poetry; it worked not through implication and juxtaposition but through assertion.

In the sonnet "On Taste" (I, 279), Clare ascribed the difference between himself and his peers to his ability to "see," which he calls taste. By taste he would seem to mean not discrimination but appreciation. He emphasizes in his sonnet that this power of apprecia-

2. *The Letters of John Clare*, eds. J. W. and Anne Tibble (London: Routledge & Kegan Paul, 1951), p. 158.
3. Ibid., pp. 256–57.
4. The problem and attitude are also evident in "An Effusion to Poesy" (I, 82) and the sonnet "Poverty" (I, 120), both written before 1819.

tion is an inspiration—"Taste is from heaven"—and that it is not something that communion with nature alone can bestow. All the country people are in close contact with natural things, "but all is night / To the gross clown."

If nature is unable to cause taste in a man, it can, nonetheless, serve as a test of it. With taste, one can read the book of nature, whose leaves would otherwise be "blank." In "Impulses of Spring" (I, 429), Clare gave this quality to his narrator, another image of himself, and thus explained his distinction from his neighbors. The experience of nature is the test of heaven-given taste, and, because he is in harmony with nature, he must possess this inspired quality. Compared with "The Village Minstrel," "Impulses of Spring" is a strident poem; the tentativeness, along with the tendency to self-pity, is replaced by self-assertion of the poetic identity. The poet is proud of his alienation, since it betokens a higher sensibility—"True poesy owns a haunted mind, / A thirst-enduring flame"—and he is contemptuous of the "rude clown of thoughtless clay," "a living blank" as he terms him. He sees now his own misery of loneliness, hardly mitigated in "The Village Minstrel," as poetic misery, the price of "feelings, blood-rushing through the soul," and the gain from it is great, the joy of poetry, which is "as the voice of God."

Clare's narrator in "Impulses of Spring" is concerned with himself as a poet, for the creation of poetry is the inevitable result of his possession of taste. Poetry is for him almost an asocial calling, requiring integrity in the poet, but not necessarily a feeling of moral responsibility to an audience, or, in fact, any commitment to a society. The villagers are dismissed in the person of the unperceiving clown, although in Clare's other poems of this period, not primarily about his poetic identity, rural society can still be portrayed as the rowdy, rude, essentially innocent world Clare felt it to be when he was not too closely involved with it.

At the end of "The Village Minstrel," Lubin was approaching manhood apprehensively, doubtful whether his poetry had merit because he was still dependent on the opinions of others. In "Impulses of Spring," nature and poetry are essential and inevitable to the poet, and there is no longer doubt about his worthiness of them. In nature and in poetry, and not among men, either those of his village or the educated ones of London who once acclaimed him, is Clare's new ideal to be found.

In the poems Clare wrote before 1821, nature is often subordinated to a human moral purpose: "His sun, sweet setting in the clearest skies, / In faith's assurance wings the soul to heaven" (I, 117). In keeping with this habit, nature is humanized, so that birds, for example, chatter and are full of "insolence and pride" (I, 182). Nature is the type of human qualities; the snowdrop as a flower becomes subordinated to the woman of whose innocence it is the "sweet type" (I, 129), and in "Langley Bush" the broken stump is "the type of broken hopes within" (II, 101).[5] At other times nature is merely the backcloth of the rural golden age, harmonizing its beauty with man's. With taste, however, nature becomes Eden itself and is less analogous to the human situation. In the process, the harmony of society and nature, a salient characteristic of the golden age, is underemphasized and then ignored, until finally it is superseded by Clare's apparent realization of the separation of society and nature.

"To the Rural Muse" (I, 449) presents a summary of Clare's ideas in the early 1820s on taste, poetry, and nature. Taste, the interpretative gift, is ascribed to the rural muse. In fact, she stands in the poem not primarily for poetry or nature, but for taste itself, and so she can make for the poet an Eden or "heaven itself" out of the common materials of the countryside. Taste does not transform nature in the way that Wordsworth's imagination does, nor is it a human emanation of emotion onto insensate objects; on the contrary, it appears to work on the human perceiver in such a way that he can see more of the beautiful in nature and in the poetry that describes it. The importance of poetry for a poet is, therefore, great, and the muse who embodies it is fittingly presented as divine in the poet's emblematic vision of her:

> I thought the very clouds around thee knelt:
> I saw the sun to linger in the west,

---

5. This poem with some emendations is reprinted by Eric Robinson and Geoffrey Summerfield in "Unpublished Poems by John Clare," *Malahat Review*, no. 2 (April 1967):112.

Paying thee worship; and as eve did melt
In dews, they seemed thy tears for sorrows I had felt.
(I, 451)

Without taste, Eden would have been merely earth, and the poet's vision commonplace; he would have "found no flowers but what the vulgar find, / Nor met one breath of living poesy," and nothing would have been covered in "dayshine," Clare's description for his vision in "The Progress of Ryhme" (*SP*, p. 116). The time of the muse's greatest visionary power is youth, and, like Wordsworth's, the poet's recollections of his vision at that time give him again something of the supreme rapturous joy he experienced in boyhood. But the power of taste can remain into manhood; the proof of its continuance is the poet's ability to see nature as Edenic and to record it in his verse.

Whether or not all receive the gift of taste in childhood is not made clear by Clare, but he is certain that some who had the faculty have perverted its use. The different types of taste men follow are described in "Shadows of Taste" (*SP*, p. 112), where they are arrayed as darkening shadows "concentring" round the natural and shining original, which is the joyful appreciation of something for its own sake. In the poem, the faculty of taste is vested in natural creatures themselves: birds, flowers, and insects "choose for joy." Man, too, "that noble insect," has taste when he sees nature as Edenic, when "Edens" appear to him "where deserts spread before." Many best find the power of taste, however, in poetry, through which "nature oer the soul her beauty flings." The taste manifested in poetry can awaken or nurture the faculty in the reader by transfixing nature for his appreciation. It makes "dashes of sunshine and a page of may," and it gathers "a blossom in its witchery of bloom."

Clare's concern in "Shadows of Taste" is not only with true taste but also with varying degrees of tastelessness. At first the man of science is contrasted with the vulgar man in his apparent appreciation of nature, but, although he does not sink to the materialism of the vulgar, the scientist does not have true taste, for his joy is from dissection, which to Clare becomes vivisection, and not from the appreciation of the whole of a living thing. His treatment of insects shows how far his gratification is from nature's innocent joy: "He unconscious gibbets butterflyes / And strangles beetles all to make us wise."[6] The man of true taste eschews cruelty, and, although his vision of nature is to some extent analytical and observational, it is also tastefully perceptive. He sees it as paradise, "wild Eden wood and field and heath," and he appreciates plants and animals as living entities in their proper homes:

> He loves not flowers because they shed perfumes
> Or butterflyes alone for painted plumes
> Or birds for singing although sweet it be
> But he doth love the wild and meadow lea
> There hath the flower its dwelling place and there
> The butterflye goes dancing through the air
> (SP, pp. 115–16).

This man of true taste is further contrasted with those who want their nature ordered and arranged according to the dictates of a human art. As with the scientist, where the excessive passion for knowledge led to a distortion of taste, here the excessive desire for order "mars the truth of taste."

Only incidentally does the poem hint at the reason so many hug the shadows and avoid the light of taste. Sometimes it is because of the distorted passion for something man-measured—order—or man-centered—wisdom. Yet another possible cause is implied in the description of the loss of beauty a plant or animal experiences if it is torn from its home within nature:

> But take these several beings from their homes
> Each beautious thing a withered thought becomes

---

6. Clare's distrust of scientific dissection occurs likewise in both the late descriptive poets and the Romantics. See William Cowper, *The Task*, in *Cowper: Poetical Works*, ed. H. S. Milford (1905; London: Oxford University Press, 1967), 3:221–24; and Keats' opinion quoted in *The Autobiography and Memoirs of Benjamin Robert Haydon*, ed. Aldous Huxley (London: Peter Davies, 1926), 1:269. Keats considered that Newton destroyed the poetry of the rainbow by reducing it to the prismatic colors. This contrasts with Thomson's much earlier enthusiasm for Newton's discoveries and dissection, recorded in his poem "To the memory of Sir Isaac Newton."

> Association fades and like a dream
> They are but shadows of the things they seem
> (SP, p. 116).

As with plants and animals, so with men. Divorced physically and mentally from their home in nature, they lose their beauty and their joyful sense of the beautiful.

According to Clare, when a man has taste and thus sees rightly, he sees nature as Eden. This idea is neither as metaphysical nor as vague as it might seem, for, although Clare, like most poets, does not define nature, it becomes clear that he is using it almost always to mean an aggregate of plants and small animals. It does not include the huge and inanimate, or the more spectacular phenomena of nature. This small circumscribed nature is Eden because it has the qualities associated with the mythological Eden, beauty and eternity, as well as the characteristics once possessed by the human society in its golden age, gentleness, kindliness, and internal harmony. The eternity nature possesses is earthly, the result of its cyclical rebirth. The same flowers blossom each spring, where man comes to his winter once and dies; thus the relative permanence of nature is contrasted with human transience. The beauty nature has is a result of its innocence. Since the human golden age has passed, it is clear that man's sin, the cause of the passing, must separate him from prelapsarian nature. Although man and nature inhabit the same earth, then, nature does not share in man's corruption, which in these poems is expressed by his pride, his cruelty, and his materialism, qualities nature does not exhibit.

"The Eternity of Nature" (SP, p. 109) is the most inclusive and typical of the many poems that deal with the theme of nature's Eden. In it, nature is the usual aggregate of flowers, animals, and insects, and the perennial character of plants is their eternity:

> . . . centurys may come
> And pass away into the silent tomb
> And still the child hid in the womb of time
> Shall smile and pluck them . . . (SP, p. 109).

Man sinned and for his sin was expelled from the place of Eden. In "The Eternity of Nature," Clare conceives of nature's accompanying man from Eden, so that the daisy now living on earth is itself Edenic, and its appearance the same as when man was innocent. Formerly its beauty might have won "een Eve to stoop adown," and

> As once in eden under heavens breath
> So now on blighted earth and on the lap of death
> It smiles for ever . . . (*SP*, p. 110).

Eden is not, then, the whole earth and its inhabitants, but the natural things that once flourished in Eden and still contain its attributes in themselves. These natural things are, of course, most Edenic where they are least touched by man.[7]

There are many proofs of the prelapsarian nature of plants and animals, their cyclical eternity and beauty the most obvious. As the there is also a mark on them, the number five, their "makers will," that sets nature apart from man as obedient and innocent. But five wounds of Christ were proof of man's redemption and Christ's divinity, so it seems here that Clare has taken the "five crimson spots" on the brow of the cowslip, the five leaves on plants, and the five eggs laid by birds as proofs of the innocence and eternity, and perhaps the redemptive power, of nature:

> And flowers how many own that mystic power
> With five leaves making up the flower
> The five leaved grass trailing its golden cups
> Of flowers . . . (*SP*, pp. 111–12).

In "The Eternity of Nature," although nature is predominantly a collection of the flowers and small animals of earth, there is a hint of another conception when Clare describes nature as the soul of these things: "Nature is their soul, to whom all clings / Of fair

---

7. Clare's emphasis on nature's prelapsarian condition may reveal the influence of Gessner's *Death of Abel*, in which Adam says at one point that only predators were expelled from Eden with him, while the gentle stayed within (p. 51).

or beautiful in lasting things." This idea may have been influenced by Wordsworth's more inclusive use of the term nature to mean both the external world and a spirit in all things. But it seems in the context of Clare's poem to be primarily a metaphorical thought, expressing the pervading attributes of nature; and Clare quickly particularizes nature again into the robin and the humble bee, whose qualities of beauty and eternity are similar, but whose souls are not a transcendent unity of the sort that a literal interpretation of the quotation would seem to suggest. In fact, it is only in the sonnet "Nature" (II, 118) that Clare holds consistently to a conception of nature as the spirit of life in natural things, a spirit that expresses the natural world's eternity and joy. But few poets are consistent in their philosophy, and it is possible to say only that the Wordsworthian view of nature as a spirit informs very few of Clare's poems and none of his major ones.

In his conception of nature's eternity, Clare remains more consistent than in his conception of nature itself. The eternity is always earthly and cyclical, not metaphysical and spiritual. Both "The Eternity of Nature" and the sonnet "Earth's Eternity" (II, 108) illustrate this. In the latter, Clare develops his theme of nature's immortality and man's transience in the light of man's prideful assumption of earth's decay, and he makes it quite clear that the eternity of earth is not a metaphysical attribute such as belongs to God, but an earthly, very long length of time. Nature's eternity, then, conquers man's idea of limited time, but it is not the sort of eternity Clare posits in another sonnet, "Eternity of Time" (II, 114), where eternity is a frightening abstraction, totally beyond the mind's comprehension. To this apocalyptic horror, nature's "eternal stay" is "but as points and commas" along the way, and the ruin of the whole earth rests easily within it: "Suns grow dark, and earth a vast and lonely tomb." But this theme of the ultimate, if far-removed, destruction of nature in a timeless eternity is a sporadic one in the period 1824 to 1832, and in most poems of this time, Clare's regard is firmly on nature in this world, its earthly eternity and Edenic beauty.

In many poems, nature's eternity and beauty are expressed in the joyful song the wind makes in the trees. This, harmonizing with the music of all living creatures, makes a universal and eternal song, important for nature because it both expresses nature's eternity and is the cause of it. The idea occurs in "Song's Eternity" (II, 266), written sometime after 1832. The surging rhythm of this poem imitates the ebb and flow of waves or the recurrent swish of the trees, all segments of nature's song:

> What is song's eternity?
>   Come and see.
> Melodies of earth and sky,
>   Here they be.
> Song once sung to Adam's ears
>   Can it be?
> Ballads of six thousand years
>   Thrive, thrive;
> Songs awakened with the spheres
>   Alive. (II, 267)

The association of the song's joy and nature's eternity is made explicit later in the poem:

> Nature's glee
> Is in every mood and tone
>   Eternity. (II, 268)

The song in this poem is continuous throughout all ages, and is the same song that existed in the first created Eden. So the joyful participation of natural things in it is another cause of their eternity and their continuing Edenic state. In *The Prelude,* 1850, Wordsworth also writes of a song of nature (II, 415–18). His treatment, however, exemplifies the difference between his and Clare's conceptions of nature. Wordsworth's song expresses the spiritual nature and unity of all things; in addition, his song is unsubstantialized, where Clare's remains an aggregate of the sounds and silences of natural things.

The song of nature is further important for its effect on man. The poet hears it when his perception is refined by taste, by poetry, and by communion with nature, and it is this too that inspires him with desire of imitation, through which he can gain for his verses a portion of the eternity that belongs to nature's song.

In "To the Rural Muse," nature's song and the young poet's verse to the rural muse are similar in their genesis. Both result from taste, which produces a joy that desires expression. When he tries to sing of his joy, therefore, the poet is joining "the anthem of the minstrel year," and is being stirred by the same rapture as the birds and trees about him:

> For summer's music in thy praise is high;
> The very winds about thy mantle sigh
> Love-melodies; thy minstrel bards to be,
> Insects and birds, exerting all their skill,
> Float in continued song for mastery;
> While in thy haunts loud leaps the little rill,
> To kiss thy mantle's hem; and how can I be still?
> (I, 451–52)

From this conception of poetic creation, it follows that the greatest achievement is to approximate both the external reality of nature and the joy of its song, and it is in this sense of a joyful imitation that Clare uses the phrase "true to nature": "Thus truth to nature as the true sublime / Stands a mount atlas overpeering time." The nearer poetic description is to the actual reality and the joy of nature, the more it will gain nature's attribute of eternity, and thus perforce have sublimity.

Clare considers, then, that poetry gains its effect by putting on the page a "pleasing image" as close to the reality of the thing in its joy as possible, a conception that is best outlined in "Shadows of Taste." Here Clare states that nature poetry should be truly descriptive in its minute particularity, but that, to be true to nature, the verse must exhibit the sort of joy nature expresses in its eternal song. For the writing of such poetry, the poet must immerse himself in the Eden of nature, keeping apart from his fellow men who do not have this joy, and he must create in himself something of the quietness and joy that are supremely nature's characteristics.

As the poet creates through taste and joy, so the reader must respond through these qualities. The true value of poetry is not in the words the poet spins but in the corresponding images that the tasteful reader can create when he reads them. This idea is most fully expressed in "Pastoral Poesy":

> True poesy is not in words,
>   But images that thoughts express,
> By which the simplest hearts are stirred
>   To elevated happiness.
>
> Mere books would be but useless things
>   Where none had taste or mind to read ... (II, 49).

This taste, which interprets the language of poetry, is of course the same quality that is required to appreciate nature. It is implied, therefore, that the joy poetry gives is the same as that given by nature, and each, nature and poetry, is described fittingly in terms of the other:

> The wild flower 'neath the shepherd's feet
>   Looks up and gives him joy;
>
> A language that is ever green,
>   That feelings unto all impart,
> As hawthorn blossoms, soon as seen,
>   Give May to every heart. (II, 49)

Poetry is, then, the human equivalent of nature's song, and should be created and responded to as nature's song. Both give the receptive person "the dower / Of self-creating joy," and both are ultimately defined through the faculty that responds to them and creates them: "Poesy's self's dwelling joy / Of humble quietness."

One would expect that Clare's insistent expression of the eternity of nature and its song should lead to a consideration of its Creator's greater eternity. Usually it does not, although in a few works of the period 1824 to 1832, there is a coupling of God with the theme of nature's immortality, a reflection perhaps of Clare's interest in religious matters during these years. Never a Christian in an orthodox and doctrinal way, Clare nonetheless appears to have given a great deal of thought to man's relations to God, especially in his frequent bouts of illness when death seemed near. His conclusions were, however, seldom lasting. In a letter to Taylor in 1823, for instance, he wrote, "I have apathy about me that looks on the powers of hells & heavens as mysterious riddles & death as an animal consequence."[8] Yet the following year, he wrote again to Taylor, "I satisfactorily prove that Religious foundation is truth & that the Mystery that envelops it is a power above human nature to comprehend."[9] In the same letter he elaborated his Protestant, undoctrinal view of religion, that, if a man satisfies his conscience and turns to God, he is sure of heaven. But Clare did not hold this faith constantly, and he soon spoke of his "dark unsettld conscience."[10]

Much of the time Clare appears to have retained some trust in a rather distant God, but clearly he disliked orthodox and institutional Christianity. Above all, his scorn is for those who measure God by man and the world, a habit which he sees as yet another example of man's incredible and selfish egocentrism. Thus he is quite clear that God is not mundane nature, since this conception would work toward elevating man to extraordinary importance. In his journal of 1824, Clare scoffs at the author of Genesis for this man- or world-centered view of God and creation: "the sacred historian took a great deal upon credit for this world when he imagines that God created the sun moon & stars those mysterious hosts of heaven for no other purpose than its use 'the greater light to rule the day & the lesser light to rule the night' and the stars also 'to give light upon the earth' it is a harmless and universal propensity to magnify consequences that appertain to ourselves."[11] Clare seems usually as certain about God's transcendence above nature as he is

8. *Letters*, p. 150.
9. Ibid., p. 159.
10. Ibid., p. 161. At this time Clare was attracted to the Nonconformist sect of the "Ranters." He admired their sincerity, although he seems to have been doubtful of their greater "zeal then knowledge," which he could not share: "O that I coud feel as they do but I cannot." See *Letters*, p. 161; Edmund Blunden, *Keats's Publisher: A Memoir of John Taylor* (1936; London: Cape, 1940), p. 173.
11. *Prose*, p. 105.

of His otherness and incomprehensibility. Occasionally there may be a wavering in this belief, as in "The Voice of Nature" (II, 39), where God gives His "own language unto nature," thus implying its Edenic qualities, and thus too allowing man to worship through attending to nature's song. This may be the Christian conception of God's gift of His Word to the world, so that man may read Him in His book of nature, an idea that seems in keeping with Clare's belief in the divine marks on nature. Yet, although Clare refers several times in his poetry to the book of nature, the book yields for him not a Christian allegory of God, but simply its own beauty.[12]

On the whole, when Clare deals with God at all, he seems to conceive of Him as outside nature. He is so in "Nature's Hymn to the Deity" (II, 83), where all parts of nature proclaim that God is with them, not of them. Also, the designation of God in this poem as "the first link in the mighty plan" seems to reveal a transcendent or ordering God rather than a Wordsworthian immanent and transcendent God. The separation is reinforced implicitly in Clare's conception of eternity that is both in time and timeless; where nature's is the former, God's is, of course, the latter.

Much more typical than the conception of God as a transcendent creator is the use of Him in a metaphoric rather than actual sense to express nature's eternity through the acknowledged eternity of its Maker. In "The Eternity of Nature," God is "that superior power" whose will has marked nature with the number five. Thus His eternity guarantees nature's while He Himself remains other than it. In one section of "The Voice of Nature," although God is often mentioned, He is not really the poet's chief concern, but rather the song of nature which is compared with His voice. At the same time His attributes lend their sublimity to nature, whose overwhelming effect on the poet is metaphorically explained:

> Though no romantic scenes my feet have trod,
> The voice of nature as the voice of God
> Appeals to me in every tree and flower,
> Breathing his glory, magnitude and power. (II, 39–40)

12. See "On Taste" and "A Morning Walk," published by Robinson and Summerfield in "Unpublished Poems by John Clare."

It is necessary to consider here the contention of Harold Bloom that, in the poems of the 1820s, Clare is derivative of Wordsworth.[13] The resemblance between Clare and Wordsworth is indeed close in their views of their poetic calling and in their total dedication to, and absorption in, poetry and nature. Thomson did not spend his life on nature poetry, and Cowper could say of himself, "But no prophetic fires to me belong; / I play with syllables, and sport in song."[14] Wordsworth, however, felt himself a spirit devoted to poetry, and Clare's dedication to his muse in "To the Rural Muse" is complete.[15] There is too a clear influence of Keats and Wordsworth on some elements of Clare's style, ranging from an occasional Wordsworthian phrase to a Keatsian use of visual personification. There may also be some influence of Wordsworth on Clare's subject matter, as in the reference in "The Eternity of Nature" to the soul of nature.

In spite of the undoubted similarities, however, it is still possible to claim that the Romantic poets, especially Wordsworth, had little effect on Clare's basic philosophy of man's separation from nature and of nature's Edenic value. Clare came to admire Wordsworth during the 1820s; in a journal entry of 1824, he wrote, "When I first began to read poetry I dislikd Wordsworth because I heard he was dislikd & I was astonishd when I lookd into him to find my mistaken pleasure in being delighted & finding him so natural & beautiful in his 'White Doe of Rylstone' there is some of the sweetest poetry I ever met with tho full of his mysteries."[16] It is the same admiration with reservation that Clare had earlier expressed for Keats' poetry. In this passage, he has separated the manner and the descriptive matter from Wordsworth's revolution-

13. *The Visionary Company*, p. 434.
14. *Table Talk*, lines 504–5.
15. Frederick W. Martin, Clare's first biographer, dramatically describes the composition of the second "To the Rural Muse" in his *Life of John Clare* (1865; London: Frank Cass, 1964). He sees it as a turning point in the poet's creative life, and he comments after his description, "It was thus a great and noble poet grew out of the 'Northamptonshire Peasant'" (pp. 237–39). Robinson and Summerfield regard this account as "perhaps the least persuasive part of the whole of Martin's *Life of John Clare*" ("Introduction," p. xxix). Nonetheless, Martin seems to have been responding to Clare's dedication of himself to poetry which is undoubtedly revealed in the poem.
16. *Prose*, p. 118.

ary philosophy, and it is in their philosophy that Wordsworth and Clare are most at odds. Clare, after *The Shepherd's Calendar*, turned his back on a social ideal and embraced one that stressed the otherness of nature; it is unlikely that he subscribed to Wordsworth's elevation of man's mind above nature, expressed both in Wordsworth's imposition of human emotion onto nature and in the explicit statements. In Book xiv of *The Prelude*, for example, the mind of man is described as "a thousand times more beautiful than the earth / On which he dwells" (lines 449–50). Similarly, Clare's conception of nature as innocent, apart from corrupted man, would make unthinkable Wordsworth's rejoicing at the sovereignty of man over nature in Book viii of *The Excursion* (lines 111–16). Indeed, in "Summer Evening" (II, 145), Clare sums up a very different view of man and nature in this way: "Thus nature's human link and endless thrall, / Proud man, still seems the enemy of all," a notion that is nearer to the older theodic philosophy than to Wordsworth's man-centered one.

The difference between Clare and Wordsworth in the matter of taste and imagination is conveniently epitomized in the Preface to the 1815 edition of the *Lyrical Ballads*. Wordsworth states that imagination endows, modifies, and creates, but does not primarily copy. In the same Preface, he quotes an opinion, with which he can disagree, of imagination as the faculty which "*images* within the mind the phenomena of sensation. . . . The imagination is formed by patient observation."[17] If the images are of Eden, as they must be from a true nature poet, this is closer to Clare's taste than to Wordsworth's imagination, for Clare said of nature that she gives man "her own imagings."[18]

In fact, Clare's conception of taste and nature, and of their relationship, resembles eighteenth-century rather than Romantic poetic thought; and, as in mode, so in philosophy he is nearer his descriptive masters. Mark Akenside, for example, whose *Pleasures of Imagination* Clare added to his library as early as 1820, stressed, like Clare, the externality of both nature and inspiration.[19] Nature

17. *The Poetical Works of Wordsworth*, ed. Thomas Hutchinson (1904; London: Oxford University Press, 1961), pp. 753–54.
18. *Prose*, p. 211.
19. *Catalogue of the John Clare Collection in the Northampton Public*

is in itself beautiful, and when selected mortals receive taste, rather like grace from above, they can appreciate and record its beauty.[20]

The difference between Clare and Wordsworth seems, then, to be based on a difference in philosophical background. Where the more subjective modern philosophy behind Wordsworth and the Romantic poets does not accept the complete autonomy of the external world, Clare's pre-Kantian way of perceiving posits a distinction between the human mind and the object, and considers that the natural object is not altered when it enters the intellectual ken of the poet.[21] When Clare posits an Eden of nature, as he had earlier a golden age society, he is positing an actual situation external to himself. Moreover, he was not receiving what he gave to it, but what it gave to him.[22] He is, therefore, implying a much more limited view of man than Wordsworth and Coleridge had, a view that asserts man's separation from, and even inferiority to, nature as well as God. Harold Bloom's assertion that much of Clare's poetry is "a postscript to Wordsworth's" is, then, erroneous, for Clare differs from Wordsworth at the very points that are most important to both poets, the conception of nature and man's relationship to it.[23]

The philosophical difference between Clare and his Romantic contemporaries results in a different selection of natural subjects. In his prose piece on landscape painting, Clare shows his realization of this fact when he records his dissatisfaction with those who select the large and grand over the beautiful and gentle. Of De Wint,

---

Library (Northampton: Public Libraries, Museums and Art Gallery Committee, 1964), p. 23.

20. *The Pleasures of Imagination* (1744), in *The Poetical Works of Mark Akenside* (London: William Pickering, 1835), 1:73–108.

21. Hence the importance of the poet himself in the Wordsworthian poem. See A. C. Bradley, "The Long Poem in Wordsworth's Age," in *Oxford Lectures on Poetry* (London: Macmillan, 1934), p. 183. Bradley asserts that the center of the Wordsworthian poem is "inward. It is an interest in emotion, thought, will, rather than in scenes, events, actions. . . ."

22. For an account of the change from the idea of art as an image of life to the idea of it as the expression of the author's temperament, see M. H. Abrams, *The Mirror and the Lamp: Romantic Theory and the Critical Tradition* (1953; New York: Norton, 1958), esp. p. 88.

23. *The Visionary Company*, p. 434.

whose paintings he approves, Clare writes, "There are no mountains lifting up the very plains with their extravagant altitudes . . . but simple woods spreading their quiet draperys to the summer sky & undiversified plains bask in the poetry of light & sunshine."[24] He praises those who make the "very copys of nature" which show the land as "a Paradise" in contradistinction to those who "imagine" and thus exaggerate aspects of nature, and those who "fancy" and thereby change the whole appearance of their subject according to their own manneristic taste.[25]

If Clare is finally un-Romantic in subject matter, so too his predominant mode remains un-Romantic, the descriptive verse of the georgic poets. In one stanza of the second "To the Rural Muse," not used in the final version, Clare wrote that "poetry lives in its simplicity, / And speaks from its own heart." To this simple poetry he contrasted bastard verse, which he described as "unmeaning music," and the kind of poetry that paints "monsters that are not and that never were." In the latter case, Clare may have been answering those who felt, with Taylor, that there was insufficient imaginative power in his verse. Clare stressed that the faculty of poetry is not that which creates something entirely from within the poet, but that which perceives Eden on earth and allows man to see common things as paradisal. He would seem to argue that he had used "taste" or imagination in his poetry, which seemed to many merely descriptive; had he not, he would have falsely described earth instead of Eden.

In the descriptive poetry Clare wrote in the late 1820s, there is rarely any of the explicit statements of nature's Edenic value that characterize the assertive poems; nonetheless, the beliefs stated in these latter works are revealed in the descriptive poems, while none of the appearance of factual truth is lost. A group of poems

---

24. *Prose*, p. 212. There was little interest in mountains in the predominantly descriptive poets of the last quarter of the eighteenth century, such as Cowper and Crabbe. The Romantic vogue for mountains accompanied a preference for wild nature and the recognition of the interpenetration of nature's life with man's. See Myra Reynolds, *The Treatment of Nature in English Poetry between Pope and Wordsworth* (1909; New York: Gordian Press, 1966), p. 342. For a later treatment of this subject, see Marjorie Hope Nicolson, *Mountain Gloom and Mountain Glory* (1959; New York: Norton, 1963).

25. *Prose*, pp. 211–12.

that exemplifies this statement exists by itself in a notebook in rough draft form. The poems deal with birds in great detail, with the sort of observational exactness Clare had asked for in his essay on De Wint's art. For the most part they are single images, realized by mainly visual description, and they work much as Clare had described poetry's functioning in "Pastoral Poesy," by causing the reader to respond with joy as he discovers for himself the joy in the visual image presented. In spite of their almost total descriptiveness, however, the poems treating bird life and lore have behind them Clare's conception of nature's innocence and immortal beauty explained in his assertive works. A walk through the woods in "The Nightingales Nest" (*SP*, p. 73), detailed as it is, becomes an entrance into the Eden of nature from which men have ejected themselves. Here the descriptive georgic method continues, but the Edenic associations elaborated in the assertive poems adhere to the details. A specific example from "The Nightingales Nest" is the description of the bird's nest:

> . . . deep adown
> The nest is made an hermits mossy cell
> Snug lie her curious eggs in number five
> Of deadened green or rather olive brown
> And the old prickly thorn bush guards them well
> And here well leave them still unknown to wrong
> As the old woodlands legacy of song (*SP*, p. 75).

In this passage, the simultaneous security and vulnerability of nature are revealed in the adverbs "deep" and "snug," and in the need for a guard. An allusion to nature's immortality is made in the mention of the number five, God's mark on nature according to "The Eternity of Nature," and the thorn bush and the woodlands are "old." Furthermore, the natural things are described as innocent, "unknown to wrong"; since the human beings are retreating, nature has still experienced no evil. The effect gained here by the philosophical associations can be seen particularly well when the poem is placed beside Clare's prose description of the same subject:

it is a very deep nest and is generaly placed on the root
or stulp of a black or white thorn somtimes a little height
up the bush and often on the ground
  they lay 5 eggs about the size of the woodlarks or
larger and of a deep olive brown (*SP*, p. 76).

As well as illustrating the concepts of the assertive poems, Clare's bird poems develop the idea of the differences between nature and man and of potential human destructiveness. The emphasis in the assertive poems on the poet's communion with nature obscured the separation of most men from nature, and the poet's ultimate inability to be at one with it. In "The Nightingales Nest," the narrator, through his memory of childhood rapture and his lack of cruelty, can penetrate some way into nature's Eden; total participation in nature is impossible for him, however, and is but one of his "happy fancys."

In the bird poems, Clare has exploited a work's need for a reader. Usually the narrator is the perceiver in the poem, and in most he leads the reader as a friend, physically accompanying him through the scenes he chooses, toward the narrator's own perception and resultant philosophy. The effect is something like a dramatic monologue, but with the reader as the recipient of the speech within the poem, an actor with a prescribed part. Thus he can be guided physically and mentally by the narrator to see with him the otherness of nature, the secrecy of her ways, and the destructiveness of man. In these poems, man is, however, still only the potential destroyer; and the reader, through the narrator who helps him to perceive this potential, is taught to restrain the destructiveness within himself. Ultimately he is persuaded to the narrator's pacific actions, as well as to his view of nature. In "The Nightingales Nest," for example, the reader is led by the narrator as his walking companion to the secret nest of the nightingale, which, unaided, he could not find. In the sequestered spot he must submit to the narrator's awe toward nature's sanctity, and learn his attitude, in the same way that he learned the path. So he must agree with his guide who says, "We will not plunder music of its dower / Nor turn this spot of happiness to thrall." The same caution is addressed to the reader by the accompanying narrator in "The Yellow-Hammer's Nest" (II, 220), where he is warned not to intrude on nature's Eden and so destroy its beauty and happiness: "Let's leave it still / A happy home of sunshine, flowers, and streams."

In all these poems, although there are few incidents given of man's cruelty to nature and no explicit statements of his radical difference from it, it is clear that natural things fear man. The existence of that fear is implied in the actions of the birds as well as in the caution of the narrator. In "The Yellow-Hammer's Nest" and "The Pettichap's Nest" (II, 219), the birds' fear of man is revealed in the initial circumstance of each poem. In the former, the bird is first seen when it is frightened by a cow-boy; in the latter, the fear is of the narrator and his companion, whose footsteps alert the bird to the alien presence of man. In "The Yellow-Hammer's Nest," too, the cruelty of man is further hinted at in the similar cruelty of snakes, another kind of creature who is not part of the Eden of small animals because of his destructiveness, and possibly also because of his part in the traditional expulsion of man from Eden.[26]

The potential cruelty of man is a mark of the difference between man and nature, a difference that often prevents man from perceiving nature correctly. Two poems in particular portray man's misunderstanding of nature and hint at the dangerous result of it. The first is "Sand Martin" (*SP*, p. 69), an address to the bird rather than to the reader, which results not in the usual poetic analogy between the poet and the bird but in a partial sharing by the poet of the ineffable feeling of nature, its "lone seclusion and a hermit joy." The innovation in this poem is the narrator's apparent distance from the poet, for, where the narrator of most of the bird poems reveals his assent to the philosophy Clare outlined in his assertive poems, the narrator here perceives nature correctly at one stage, but apparently not throughout the poem. A measure of this vacillation is the repeated word "lone":

26. In the few bird poems where the narrator is walking alone, the menaced security of nature is still a theme, but there is more emphasis on nature's nonhuman paradise, for the narrator is seemingly less of a threat than other men. See "Pewits Nest" (*SP*, p. 82), and "The Yellow Wagtail's Nest" (II, 223).

Ive seen thee far away from all thy tribe
Flirting about the unfrequented sky
And felt a feeling that I cant describe
Of lone seclusion and a hermit joy
To see thee circle round nor go beyond
That lone heath and its melancholy pond
(SP, p. 69).

The first time "lone" is used it helps to describe the empathetic feeling the poet has with nature; it is thus an appreciative adjective. The second time, it aids the process of distancing the speaker, and therefore the reader, from the natural object, so that, as a description of merely human perception at this stage, it has a pejorative association. "Lone" also echoes the opening of the poem, which presents the human view of the sand martin's home:

Thou hermit haunter of the lonely glen
And common wild and heath—the desolate face
Of rude waste landscapes far away from men
(SP, p. 69).

This view is transformed only as the poet comes to feel "the desolate face" of nature as "a hermit joy." At the end, the desolate place is once again "that lone heath and its melancholy pond." Earlier coupled with joy, "lone" is now linked with melancholy; so there seems to be a movement within the speaker of the poem from the solely human regard of nature to the joy-producing human contact with nature and then back to the merely human perception of the wasteland. Nature's reality, and man's response to it, are therefore contrasted within the changing attitude of the speaker as he moves near to nature and then away from it. The bird's joy in the wasteland is felt for a moment by the poet, and his perception is doubled, but the melancholy loneliness intrudes, and he returns to his single human perception.

In the second poem, "The Sky Lark" (SP, p. 77), it is not the narrator who is deficient in perception but the schoolboys. The reader is exhorted to watch as if he were a bystander as the skylark flies up from the nest. The scene of this poem is set not through a broad description of the countryside and sky, but through a selection of small details that suggest the overall scene, almost as if Clare were immediately reminding the reader that nature is a collection of the small details of the earth:

> The rolls and harrows lies at rest beside
> The battered road and spreading far and wide
> Above the russet clods the corn is seen
> Sprouting its spirey points of tender green
> Where squats the hare to terrors wide awake
> Like some brown clod the harrows failed to break
> (SP, p. 77).

The focus moves here through the cornfield to the hare, who has the terror of all small things of nature, as well as their kinship with the earth, the clods of the field. The hare becomes an epitome of all frightened animals, then, and when the skylark is introduced one can assume her characteristics from this description of her fellow creatures. After this setting of the scene, the schoolboys enter, the human element coming to raid nature. They surprise the skylark, whose subsequent flight and joy in the sky they see, but not her fall:

> ... the sky lark flies
> And oer her half formed nest with happy wings
> Winnows the air till in the clouds she sings
> Then hangs a dust spot in the sunny skies
> And drops and drops till in her nest she lies
> (SP, p. 77).

The rest of the poem concentrates on the typical reaction of the boys to the bird. Not understanding her harelike characteristics, they cannot believe in her earthliness, but consider her "free from danger as the heavens are free / From pain and toil." They imagine her going "about the world to scenes unheard / Of and unseen":

>   ... —O where they but a bird
>   So think they while they listen to its song
>   And smile and fancy and so pass along
>   While its low nest moist with the dews of morn
>   Lies safely with the leveret in the corn (*SP*, pp. 77–78).

Through his narrator who has seen the hare and the bird and the clods of earth, Clare seems to be contrasting two ways of perceiving nature. Through the first, the narrator realizes its otherness, its fear of man; and in the low nest of the skylark he understands the earthliness and vulnerability of the bird and of all natural things. The second is a purely human, man-centered notion of the animal world, and this the boys show when they unsubstantialize the bird because they do not really see her. In fact they have "unheeding past" the skylark on her nest, and they are thus seeing the bird only partially when they see her in flight. Even then, she becomes not a bird above her nest, but their own aspirations materialized; their "fancy" ignores the real terror and vulnerability of the bird, as well as the careful joy in her nest. This sort of joy, it is implied, they could not understand, for, although they have come merely to pluck the buttercups, it is the same urge that motivates boys in other poems to plunder birds' eggs, and, finally, men to destroy trees and hedges in enclosure.[27]

"The Sky Lark" is very close in its description of the boys' response to Shelley's "To a Skylark," in which the bird becomes an insubstantial symbol of the poet's emotions:

>   With thy clear keen joyance
>   Languor cannot be:
>   Shadow of annoyance
>   Never came near thee. (lines 76–79)

By the side of this and many similar examples of Wordsworth's poetry, such as "To the Cuckoo," it is hard to avoid seeing Clare's poem as in some way answering the Romantic tendency to regard

---

27. See "Wild Duck's Nest" (II, 343) and "A Favourite Nook Destroyed" (I, 531).

the human response to, and not the reality of, an object, and at the same time to avoid acknowledging in this response man's insensitivity to real nature and his cruelty to it.[28]

In 1827, Clare wrote to his friend George Darley, "My judgment some years back was as green as a child's in matters of taste & now I think it is ripened & good."[29] The poems of the last half of the 1820s show Clare's confidence in his own taste, in his subject matter, and in its treatment. His predominant descriptive mode continues in his bird poems and in his numerous other vignettes of natural things; but, in the best, the mode has been modified by the philosophical assertive poems in such a way that it has gained, without sacrificing observational accuracy, some of the philosophical and emotional depth that Taylor felt was lacking in Clare's work. The bird poems extend not so much our understanding of nature's Eden as man's relationship to it. They present his correct attitude of joyful contemplation and reverence, and at the same time show his man-centered view and his destructiveness, which are threats to Eden.

The vision of nature as Eden was seemingly a more satisfying answer to Clare's quest for an ideal than his conception of a social golden age had been. So he can be more assertive of it in his philosophical poems. Also, the Eden of nature he posits is free from the internal tension of the human ideal, and can, therefore, be embraced more wholeheartedly. The difficulty in it is the difficulty of Clare's conception of Eden as actual, physical, and earthly: it is susceptible to the human society which he has repudiated. The potential danger is one message of the bird poems, for not all human intruders into nature will be as cautious and as reverent as Clare's narrator.

28. Raynor Unwin contrasts the Romantic with the peasant attitude to external nature. Where many of the Romantics saw nature as ancillary to man, the peasant poets exhibited "an unselfconscious humility towards external nature, bred from the respect that close association often imparts" (p. 35).
29. *Letters*, p. 202.

4
The Loss of Eden

In *The Shepherd's Calendar,* Clare had expressed his golden age ideal and in the process revealed his dissatisfaction with it. The reason for his inability to retain a social standard was initially his nearness to the reality from which the earlier writers of a rural golden age had been divorced by location or situation. Later, his residual belief in the ideal was further and more drastically eroded by his realization that the enclosure movement had destroyed whatever attributes he had prized in his society. He therefore turned from it increasingly after 1824 to find his positive standard in the Eden of small things, in which he saw the qualities of freedom, humility, gentleness, and harmony now lost by human society, as well as the nonhuman attributes of eternity, secrecy, and pristine innocence. Yet, during the last few years of the 1820s, Clare realized that the enclosure movement, which had impinged at first primarily on his fellow peasants and their immediate surrounds, was as well the destroyer of this Edenic nature. His attitude to the movement that had been a frequent subject in his verses from his earliest poetic years became more deeply hostile. At the same time the change enclosures had wrought became for him all-embracing. The result was an erosion of his confidence even in a harmony between nature and those selected men who could appreciate if not experience the Eden of nonhuman things. For Clare, then, the enclosure movement marked the end of man's communion with nature's Eden and a proof of his total depravity.

The decline from the golden age started when death came into the world and man first tilled the soil, but it gained impetus only in Clare's own time. This decline is rarely imaged by Clare as a fall. Yet the depravity of man seems to be in the background of the Edenic nature poems, for man's potential destructiveness and his contrast with nature's innocence both indicate that he has fallen and been separated from Edenic nature. The imagery of the fall, however, is reserved by Clare for describing the loss of taste or perception that man experiences some time after the original exile from Eden. To put it another way, the loss of the golden age, one of whose characteristics is the harmony of man and nature, is followed by man's inability to perceive even the harmony of nature. Driven from Eden, he eventually loses sight of it completely, and it is for this loss that Clare reserves the dramatic imagery of the fall of man.

To observe how the enclosure movement could have come to affect Clare and his poetic faith so deeply, it is necessary to appreciate its importance to a village such as Clare inhabited. Enclosure in the eighteenth and early nineteenth centuries is defined by R. A. C. Parker as two processes: "One was the rationalization of the open field system with its sometimes complicated rights of pasturage, the second was the bringing into cultivation or into more intensive cultivation of land hitherto uncultivated or lightly cultivated."[1] The process was stimulated by improved agricultural methods in the eighteenth century and by the high price of agricultural produce, particularly during the French wars, that made it profitable to enclose lands, even by the expensive means of enclosure by parliamentary act.[2] The amount of land enclosed varied from county to county, but Gonner has calculated that the two counties most affected by acts on open-field arable land were Huntingdonshire and Clare's county of Northamptonshire with over 50 per cent of this land enclosed.[3]

The complex effects of enclosures, particularly on the poorer social elements, have been the subject of great controversy. For

1. *Enclosures in the Eighteenth Century* (London: Routledge & Kegan Paul for the Historical Association, 1960), p. 3.
2. In 1801 there was a general enclosure act, after which private acts were passed in accordance with its provisions; but enclosure remained a costly process. See E. C. K. Gonner, *Common Land and Inclosure* (1912; New York: Kelley, 1966), pp. 59–60, 201.
3. Ibid., pp. 268–69. Parker points out that Gonner's statistics are flawed, first because they were based on estimates in the acts, not in the more reliable awards, and second because the areas counted included much common or waste land (p. 9). The figures may, however, be taken as approximations.

Clare, however, they appeared simply a degeneration. The exploitation of nature destroyed the necessary equilibrium of man and his environment, and the change in the pattern of cultivation caused a change in village life, disrupting the social harmony and equality Clare felt had been rural characteristics since early times. Experiencing, then, neither social nor economic gains from enclosures and conceiving of none, Clare supports in his treatment of the movement the gloomy picture of the poor painted by J. L. and Barbara Hammond in *The Village Labourer*.[4] Many scholars have doubted the dramatic conclusions of the Hammonds, and certainly some of their economic arguments have not withstood the criticisms and discoveries of modern scholars.[5] Yet these scholars, by regarding enclosure in Gonner's words as "a part of a wider economic movement" and by focusing on the economic aspect alone, perhaps lost the intensity of the peasant experience in the search for economic perspective.[6] From the vantage of several recent findings, Clare's response to enclosure may appear excessive, or, more accurately, a reaction not simply to enclosure but to the complex of economic, social, and philosophical changes causing widespread poverty in the early nineteenth century, of which he took enclosure as the cause. However, judged by the facts he records in his *Sketches* and by contemporary accounts of the victims of enclosure, which the Hammonds use in their study, his strong response to the movement seems appropriate.[7] I shall briefly summarize the Hammonds' arguments where they seem essentially a

4. (1911; London: Longmans, 1966). G. E. Mingay, in his introduction to the 1966 edition of Gonner's work, calls the Hammond view "basically the Marxist one of expropriation and expulsion" (p. xliii). Marx saw enclosure playing a central role in the emergence of the capitalist farmer and in the transformation of the peasantry into the urban proletariat. See *Capital*, ed. F. Engels (1867; New York: Random House, 1936), pp. 788–816.

5. The lines of the enclosure debate were drawn early in this century. The main opponents of the Hammonds were Gonner and A. H. Johnson, whose conclusions suggested that agricultural changes in the late eighteenth and early nineteenth centuries were not as radical as Marx and the Hammonds supposed. The debate continues, although many modern scholars, such as Mingay, H. J. Habbakkuk, and J. D. Chambers, have largely accepted the economic conclusions of Gonner and Johnson.

6. *Common Land and Inclosure*, p. vi.

7. J. H. Clapham implies that the Hammonds frequently generalize from atypical and minority instances. See *An Economic History of Modern Britain* (Cambridge: At the University Press, 1926), p. 119. However, both Par-

discursive statement of Clare's attitudes, and indicate some of the more important disagreements of their critics.

Basically, the Hammonds' view is that, in the late eighteenth and early nineteenth centuries, the age-old enclosure movement became a revolution, radically affecting the social and economic situations of the poor; that the poor were transformed from an independent class into enforcedly servile laborers; and that the injustice and hardship attendant on enclosure were in the main unnecessary. In addition, they emphasize the ecological and social losses as well as the economic loss of the peasants, a point little discussed by Gonner, their most influential opponent.

The enclosing of the land, segmenting the open moorland, physically altered the environment of the peasants. Field work, neither as communal nor as open as before, became more monotonous; cultivators turned into hired laborers; and the link between work and enjoyment, as expressed in the village rites that had once been a part of rural life, was broken. The disappearance of the festivals and frolics that marked Clare's golden society, a process chronicled in *The Shepherd's Calendar,* was due both to this changing peasant status and to the increasing poverty.[8] In addition, the composition of the village community itself changed. There had been, in the old villages with their fairly stable populations, very few landless laborers without common rights, and, although not all had actually been equal, there had been on the whole a possible and proper pride for all elements, with a resultant sense of independence even for the poorest.[9] This independence was, however, ultimately connected with rights, such as those of grazing and gleaning, and it

---

ker (p. 7) and the Hammonds (p. 334) point out that the poorer classes left few records.

8. J. D. Chambers has suggested that the rural poverty of the early nineteenth century was caused not primarily by enclosure, as the Hammonds suggest, and poor law measures, as Karl Polanyi claims in *The Great Transformation* (1944; Boston: Beacon Press, 1968), but by factors causing poverty throughout the country: the rise in population, war conditions, and the postwar depression. See "Enclosure and Labour Supply in the Industrial Revolution," *Economic History Review,* 2d ser., 5 (1952–53):319–43.

9. See G. Slater, *The English Peasantry and the Enclosure of Common Fields* (Oxford: Oxford University Press, 1907) for the view that in the open village the laborer without land and rights was scarcely to be found (p. 130). Mingay regards this view, on later evidence, as untenable, and he

was of these rights that cottagers like Clare's father were deprived, usually without adequate compensation.[10]

The measures to deal with the social upheaval of the enclosure years equaled in their unpleasant results the enclosures themselves.[11] The miseries of the newly dispossessed were augmented by the Speenhamland System, called by the Hammonds "a universal system of pauperism."[12] The makers of this act, rejecting the idea of a minimum wage and allotments for the poor, proposed that the deficient wages of laborers be brought up to subsistence level by parish relief. Through this system the last remnant of independence was taken from the poor, who became paupers whatever their efforts.[13] At the same time, the French wars caused shortages and soaring rents, so that more people than ever were thrown totally onto the degrading charity of the parish. For these people the workhouse was established to replace the parish houses, and it became at once an institution dreaded by the poor, no less for the degradation it implied than for the dirt and disease encountered there.[14] Other evils added to the harshness of the system. The church tithes that should have been used for poor relief seldom

---

describes it as essentially Marxist romanticism (Introduction to Gonner, pp. xl–xli).

10. Confirmation for this connection comes from the *Report on Shropshire* made in 1794 by a Mr. Bishton: "The use of common land by labourers operates upon the mind as a sort of independence" (quoted in *The Village Labourer*, p. 31). Gonner denies the injustice: "It seems true that the compensation given was equal in value to the rights of which they were deprived" (p. 367). Yet most writers admit the Hammonds' point that there was no compensation where rights were shadowy and the claimant unassertive, and that the poorer cottagers frequently suffered, especially from the loss of commons and wastes (*Enclosures in the Eighteenth Century*, p. 13; *Common Land and Inclosure*, p. 368).

11. Gonner denies the causative connection made by the Hammonds between enclosure and increased but harsher poor relief (pp. 415–19). Clare usually juxtaposes enclosure with harsher treatment of the poor, both being caused by the more affluent social elements. See "The Sorrows of Love" (I, 466) and "The Parish" (I, 562).

12. *The Village Labourer*, p. 162.

13. Frederic Morton Eden claims that, if a minimum wage had been enforced in place of parish relief, the laborer "would have considered it as his right, and not as charity; and the spirit of independence, now almost extinct, would have been preserved and cherished." See *The State of the Poor*, ed. A. G. L. Rogers (1797; London: Routledge, 1928), p. 121.

14. Eden gives several examples of inappropriate buildings and dirty conditions, often resulting in fever epidemics (pp. 373, 254, 286).

were, and the Anglican Church, which had become part of the landed establishment, was of little comfort to its less fortunate members.[15] With private ownership of commons and heaths, trespassing and game laws became more numerous and more ferocious in their penal clauses, as poverty and thus the temptation of poaching increased.[16]

In 1809 the Act of Parliament of '49 Geo III was passed for enclosing lands in several parishes of Northamptonshire; among them were Northborough, where Clare was to move in 1832, and Helpston, his home for most of his life. Although the actual enclosure award for Helpston bears the date 1820, many of the changes that are associated with enclosure were taking place between 1809 and 1820. The movement therefore accompanied Clare's own development during these years from relatively happy youth to impoverished and insecure maturity, and offers a parallel to it.

In Clare's early childhood, his father, Parker Clare, was a flail-thresher, receiving 8s a week.[17] On this he could satisfactorily keep his wife and two children. When Clare was about twelve, however, Parker Clare became so weakened by rheumatism that his son had to work to support the household.[18] Yet as enclosures crept on, agricultural work appeared increasingly elusive, and the young Clare took any work available to battle the poverty that was already closing in on him.[19] He was, for example, a limeburner at one

---

15. *The Village Labourer*, p. 165. See also Adam Smith, *The Wealth of Nations* (1776; New York: Collier, 1905), 3:243; and W. R. Ward, "The Tithe Question in England in the Early Nineteenth Century," *Journal of Economic History* 16 (April 1965):67–81.

16. *The Village Labourer*, p. 333. See Clare's fear of trespassing in "Trespass" (II, 373) and his account of his near arrest for poaching, which ends: "What terrifying rascals these woodkeepers & gamekeepers are they make a prison of the forrests & are its gaolers" (*Prose*, p. 143).

17. *Life*, p. 8. This appears a normal wage for a laborer at the time since the amount is mentioned also in Eden, p. 123.

18. Clare wrote that he had some schooling when his father was well: "I think never a year pass'd me till I was 11, or 12, but 3 months or more at the worst of times was luckily spared for my improvement" (*Sketches*, p. 48).

19. Eden and the Hammonds contend that unemployment was caused by the destruction of the old village bureaucracy, by the transformation of poor farmers into laborers, by the change from arable land to pasture through enclosure when it occurred, and by the sudden fall in prices at the end of the war (*The Village Labourer*, pp. 94, 97, 171). Gonner, on the other hand, con-

time, and at another a member of a "catchwork gang," a group of dispossessed laborers who hired themselves out indiscriminately.[20]

As the hard times continued, Clare's family sank into deep financial distress. On his return home from work in another village, Clare found his father reduced through ill health and unemployment to the condition of a pauper, earning his weekly 5s from the parish by roadmending.[21] On another occasion, he found his family on the verge of being moved to the parish house for paupers.[22] But the enclosure movement affected Clare and his family more than financially; it caused emotional deprivation by the restraint it put on the communion with nature, so that the happiness Clare had found as a child in woods and heaths was curtailed. By 1816, parts of Helpston Heath were being plowed up, and trees like Round Oak and Lea Close Oak, which Clare knew by name, were being felled.[23]

After Clare's literary success in 1820, a small annuity was procured for him by his patrons, but it amounted to roughly what he would have earned as a day laborer, and, with a growing family and his parents to support, his financial situation was little improved. During the next decade, frequent bouts of illness and growing evidence of mental sickness, in addition to the worsening economic situation of all agricultural laborers, made it impossible for him to break out of the cycle of poverty and debt into which he had been born.

Of the few poets who record the rural change caused by the enclosure movement—primarily Goldsmith in *The Deserted Village*, Crabbe in *The Village, The Borough*, and *The Parish Register*, Barnes in his eclogues, and Clare—only Clare is truly of the class

---

cludes there could have been little overall fall in employment through enclosure considering the work it entailed (pp. 396–402), and that there was no notable diminution of arable land through enclosure at this time. Clare's county of Northamptonshire, however, was most heavily affected by the conversion, at least before 1800 (pp. 400–401).

20. *Life*, pp. 31, 42.

21. *Sketches*, p. 70. Clare says that his father worked for his weekly 5s "fancying he was not so much beholden to their forced generosity, as if he had taken it for nothing." The loss of self-respect the parish charity caused is stressed by Eden (p. 125).

22. *Life*, p. 51.

23. Ibid., p. 41.

he describes and is thus experiencing and observing at first hand the peasants' hardships.[24] He too is the only one for whom the enclosure movement is of more than peripheral interest. Thus when Clare deals with the effects of enclosures on the poor, as in his long satiric description, "The Parish," he does so in bitter detail, producing a poem harsher in its treatment of the ruling parish elite than anything by Crabbe or Barnes. He stresses that peasant suffering has resulted from the cupidity of the landowners, and he consequently responds to them with hatred.

Since enclosures were in Clare's view obliterating the social and physical surroundings of his youth, it is to be expected that they should figure largely in his earliest verse. It is not, however, until "The Parish: A Satire" (I, 542), written mainly between 1820 and 1824, that Clare explored the detailed effects of the enclosing movement on a village community. The text of the poem printed by J. W. Tibble is neither complete nor definitive, and there appear to be several places where the order of sections is suspect; but the poem is full enough as it stands to reveal Clare's characteristic method of juxtaposition, here a series of character sketches of the corrupt present with other sketches or passing allusions indicating the pristine goodness of the past age.[25]

It becomes clear early in the poem that the present society prizes and exhibits qualities opposite to those that made the golden age of rural England pleasant and joyful. The harmony of social elements, their essential equality, the independence and freedom of

---

24. A few other poets deal in passing with rural misery, although they rarely take enclosure as the cause. Cowper, for example, in *The Task*, sees something of the peasants' suffering, but considers it mostly "th'effect of laziness or sottish waste" (IV, 431). Most of the writers who deal fully with enclosure deflect blame for rural suffering from the land-owning class. Goldsmith blamed merchants and manufacturers, while Wordsworth blamed the new factory system. See Kenneth Maclean, *Agrarian Age: A Background for Wordsworth* (New Haven: Yale University Press, 1950), pp. 32–38, 95.

25. Clare used the heroic couplet for his satiric description, and was much influenced by earlier users, such as Pope and Crabbe. Clare read Pope's poetry (*Letters*, p. 30), and, on completing his own satire, quoted Pope in support of his claim to general, not specific, criticism (*Letters*, p. 140). In a letter of 1820 to Taylor, Clare wrote "I imitate Crabb," but he added, "Whats he know of the distresses of the poor musing over a snug coal fire in his parsonage box" (*Letters*, p. 75).

the people, their energetic kindness and care were the earlier golden age qualities that are now despised or forgotten. "The Parish" thus becomes an exaggeration of the hints of degeneration given in *The Shepherd's Calendar,* and the obverse of its golden picture of rural harmony and happiness.

In the post-enclosure world of "The Parish," the motivating force of the people, and so of the enclosure movement, is pride, a pride that no longer means independence and liberty, but is rather a synonym for tyranny, a pride that needs for its expression the subordination of another. This pride causes the parish officers' assertion of their authority over the weak, as well as the social aspirations of the farmers. The result of the transformation of prosperous farmers into gentry is at first the degradation of their hired laborers and subsequently the corruption of words such as "free" and "equal" when applied to these laborers.[26] The enclosers talk much of "freedom," and the final irony for Clare is that the enslavement of the peasants and the land should be done in its name. The perversion of language is extended to all words that once had good and beneficial referents: "religion" becomes synonymous with "cant," "justice" with "injustice" and "interest." This linguistic degeneration, from Thucydides onward the mark of moral decline in a nation, accompanies a speech that is divorced from action, a probable reason for Clare's dislike of vocal reformers. It is, indeed, the politician in "The Parish" whose speech is most marked by perversity. Praising equality, he "stints the pauper of his parish fare," and, canting of freedom, he enslaves those below him: "Thus freedom-preaching is but knavery's game / And old self-interest by another name."

One common device of satire used in "The Parish" is revealed by the use of the word "ape" to describe the actions and attitudes of the new race of men, as if in aspiring to be what they should not

---

26. The connection Clare makes between these two metamorphoses is made also by Cobbett in his *Political Register* of 1821: "The life of the husbandman cannot be that of a *gentleman* without injury to society at large. When farmers become *gentlemen* their labourers become *slaves*. A *Virginian* farmer, as he is called, very much resembles a *great farmer* in England" (quoted in Hammond, p. 210). The loss of intimacy between farmer and laborer because of the new wealth and status of the farmers is a major theme too of Robert Bloomfield's *Farmer's Boy,* 1800.

they become subhuman. The farmer's daughter, now ashamed of her rustic situation and her wealth based on land, is "aping" wit; and Farmer Thrifty, Headlong Racket, and the village officers all "ape" what they basely aspire to. In addition, there are reductive comparisons of these people with other sorts of animals, all either domestic, man-controlled, or unpleasant, and so not a part of Clare's Eden of natural things. Headlong Racket, for example, leads a life that is subhuman in its uselessness, as he "prepares by turns to hunt and whore and shoot, / Less than a man and little more than brute." Dandy Flint becomes "a dirty hog that on the puddle's brink / Stirs up the mud and quarrels with the stink," and all the newborn race of tyrants is summed up as "things that o'er inferiors flirt, / That spring from pride like summer flies from dirt."[27] Men are degraded by these bestial comparisons, and there is the implication that they have broken from their proper place in the scheme of things and, by aspiring beyond themselves, have fallen downward. The imagery here reinforces Clare's idea that enclosure is destroying a natural order by making man supreme in a world in which human supremacy indicates only corruption and perversity.

The idea of the unseemliness, the unnaturalness or gracelessness, of the new age is expressed again in the character sketch of the farmer's daughter, who, like Cowper's rural lass in Book IV of *The Task*, is metamorphosed into the fashionable lady. Once she milked the cows and was "as red and rosy as the lovely spring." This is the description of a golden age maiden, as in *The Shepherd's Calendar*, for example, who is in tune with nature and is like the flowers and pleasant seasons. Now, in the new era, this link with nature is destroyed, and the girl becomes "pale," "a formal shade," her sunny brightness gone. She has moved away from nature, forsaken the cows, and divorced herself from the natural operation of the seasons: thus she is afraid of "vulgar winds." This separation is emphasized by her new occupation; now no longer like a flower herself, she "paint[s] unnatural daubs of fruit or flower."

The character sketches of "The Parish" move down the hierarchy of notables, exemplifying each parochial institution and its peculiar

27. The Popean echoes in "The Parish" are strongest in these reductive comparisons.

degeneration. One attribute shared by all the parish notables is the possession of wealth, a necessity for office or status in the new world. Money becomes the measure of all men, and gold can substitute for almost all the qualities that once were valued:

> Gold is a mighty substitute—it buys
> The fool sufficient credit to seem wise,
> The coward laurels, virtue unto bawds,
> A mask for villainy and fame for lords;
> Buys knaves an office, traitors trust and power;
> Buys lies and oaths, and breaks them every hour;
> Buys cant its flattery, hypocrites their paint,
> Making a very devil seem a saint;
> Buys asses panegyrics and what not,
> And makes man worshipped and leaves God forgot;
> In fact, buys all and everything, forsooth,
> But two poor outcasts—honesty and truth. (I, 557-58)

The complement of this situation is the treatment of poverty not as a misfortune but as a crime. The workhouse, "a makeshift shed of misery," is set up for the oppression, not the aid, of the poor, since "'twas not contrived for want to live, but die." Fittingly, then, the place faces the cold north, is gardenless, and shuttered, so that indignity and misery may be joined to the poverty of the inmates:

> Here dwell the wretched, lost to hopeless strife,
> Reduced by want to skeletons in life,
> Despised by all . . . (I, 564).

The poor become "harmless flocks" to the parish "dogs," who, all-powerful here, "feel no mercy where they fear no bite."

Throughout "The Parish" the character sketches of the new order are measured against sketches of, or allusions to, the pleasanter society of the past. The longest positive section is the standard provided for religion, a rather Goldsmithian sketch of the old vicar from "days gone by." A man "plain as the flock dependent on his cares," he avoided the greed of the later age by living in a plain house, a situation that emphasized his association with the majority of his parishioners instead of with the gentry. He had, too, retained his link with nature; unlike his successors, he kept no dogs "to run the harmless hare," and his garden's crop of "pinks and roses" is in sharp contrast to its present one of "docks and nettles," appropriate for an age that does not value natural things. Only the politician in the Tibble text is measured by no positive standard from the past. Perhaps this is because Clare felt the breed to be a new one, peculiarly dependent upon the new age and having no counterpart in a purer one.

Except for the section on the old vicar, the positive passages of "The Parish" are muted. This, added to the intensity and directness of the sketches, gives an effect very different from that of Crabbe's social poems. The difference, no doubt, is due in part to the genesis of Clare's poem: "This poem was begun and finished under the pressure of heavy distress, with embittered feelings under a state of anxiety and oppression almost amounting to slavery, when the prosperity of one class was founded on the adversity and distress of the other" (I, 542). It is not surprising to find that Crabbe, whose primary interest was the recording of human nature, should have produced in *The Borough* sketches that are rounded and complex where Clare's in "The Parish" are usually flat, uniform, and vindictive—so vindictive indeed that the effect is to leave an impression of the author's unrelenting bitterness toward, and hatred of, the exploiter of social evils rather than any clear vision of the exploiters or the evils he rails against. Yet this impression was perhaps part of his aim. "The Parish" conveys Clare's "embittered feelings" and, therefore, gives a picture not only of rural despotism but of the response of a dispossessed peasant to it.

The effects on society of the enclosure movement and its economic accompaniments were deeply felt by Clare. Yet his growing preoccupation with nature during the 1820s ensured that his deepest response would be reserved for nature's suffering. His conception of nature as Eden, innocent and eternal, makes its enslavement and destruction both a sacrilege and a certain proof of human depravity, even more than man's enslavement of his fellows. For Clare there was no justification for extending cultivated land: in the ordered society of the golden age there has been a sufficiency for all, and the extension was thus due solely to man's greed and impious desire for domination. Clare's short poem "The Mores" (*SP*, p. 169) expressed the implications of this domination, and made the enclosure movement a complex yet unified catastrophe befalling men and the land in common.

In "The Mores," Clare forces the reader, by his juxtaposition of the present with the past, nature's Eden with the result of man's willful destruction of it, to realize the enormity of the loss resulting from enclosure. As usual there is no compromise, no hint that the plow's ravaging does not destroy the land's purity forever or that the enclosure movement could have anything but a disastrous effect on man and nature. The various ties are severed, between heaven and earth, man and nature, age and childhood, rich and poor. No group gains from the severance, and, even for the rich, nature's exploitation will in time be self-defeating.

The contrast of the pre-enclosure and post-enclosure worlds is made through the condition of the moorlands. Once they were free, "unbounded," "uncheckt," and "undwarfed" by bush and tree. They reflected and imitated the heavens, and in blossom resembled "fallen landscapes from an evening sky." They were the supreme example of eternity and infinity on earth:

> Far spread the moorey ground a level scene
> Bespread with rush and one eternal green
> That never felt the rage of blundering plough
> Though centurys wreathed springs blossoms on its brow
> . . . .
> Its only bondage was the circling sky
> One mighty flat undwarfed by bush and tree
> Spread its faint shadow of immensity (*SP*, p. 169).

The contrasting man-controlled land is broken into segments, and the appearance of spatial hugeness of the moors is destroyed:

> ... sky bound mores in mangled garbs are left
> Like mighty giants of their limbs bereft

> Fence now meets fence in owners little bounds
> Of field and meadow large as garden grounds
> In little parcels little minds to please
> With men and flocks imprisoned ill at ease (*SP*, p. 170).

The link with heaven was broken when the land was mutilated, and the rupture was ratified by man's mark of ownership that "shows where man claims earth glows no more divine."

As the land was mutilated, so were the men and animals on it. In the pre-enclosure world, they lived in harmony with natural events; the cows and sheep came and went with the morning and evening appropriately, and the shepherd was as "free as the lark and happy as her song." The division was not yet distinct between man and his subject animals, and wild nature that lived according to the times of day and the seasons of the year. Also there is the implication that nature provided adequately for all when all lived in proper relationship with her without greed:

> Cows went and came with evening morn and night
> To the wild pasture as their common right
> And sheep unfolded with the rising sun
> Heard the swains shout and felt their freedom won
> Tracked the red fallow field and heath and plain
> Then met the brook and drank and roamed again (*SP*, p. 170).

Enclosure destroyed both man's right relationship with nature and the harmony between men. The freedom of the poor was lost: "Inclosure came and trampled on the grave / Of labours rights and left the poor a slave." In addition, Clare associated the freedom of the land and the creatures dwelling on it with their joy and with the time of childhood when men shared that joy. When the link between man and nature was destroyed, along with rural freedom, so was joy, both its past existence and any future possibility. Although, then, the economic and social losses of the peasants are a concern in "The Mores," a greater one is the moral and spiritual loss man and the land sustain.

"The Mores" indicates that Clare, unlike Goldsmith and Barnes, saw the enclosure movement not merely as a cultural, social, and economic change, but as a universal moral decline that could be compared imaginatively to the fall and expulsion from Eden. The movement destroyed all that he valued in his rural society and obliterated the tenuous links between man and nature, and thus man's ability to perceive and participate in the Eden that nature had been until that time. In addition, enclosures exalted the materialism and cruelty that had been latent in his society, and raised man to the supreme position on earth, keeping him there by the enslavement of the natural things that had once held the earth in trust with him. It is not surprising, then, that the shock of enclosures should have caused in Clare a total distrust of man and a complete pessimism concerning the future.

The seriousness of the moral disaster led Clare to examine the manifestation of man's fallen nature in relatively simple human acts. "The Destroyer" (II, 283), written some time after 1832, is one such examination. Nature comes forth in its bloom and beauty to be met not by the greedy exploiter but by the simple shepherd, who "with almost every footstep crushed a flower":

> The winds did all they could, though oft in vain,
> To raise and form them on their stalks again,
> . . . .
> And those his dog beat down did hardly mind
> But formed again as happy as the wind,
> Leaving a lesson sad with every day
> That harm falls most in man's destroying way:
> And who could think in such a lovely time
> And such a spot, where quiet seemed in prime,
> As ne'er to be disturbed, that strife and fear
> Like crouching tigers had howled havoc here? (II, 283)

In this short poem, Clare shows that his long contemplation of the destructiveness of enclosures has attuned him to the constant tendency to cruelty in man, a tendency which he can never escape or eradicate.

All the enclosure poems so far mentioned have revealed Clare's mode as predominantly the georgic descriptive one. In them, the reader, presented with the selected, external phenomena, is not on the whole urged by the poet to respond emotionally or imaginatively. In "The Destroyer," this unassertive, undemanding description is used in the first few lines. Toward the end, however, the appearance of some detachment that such description needs is replaced by the assertive, emotionally demanding mode of Clare's philosophical poems; the use of the rhetorical question, rare in Clare, enforces the change. Considering the close relationship of Clare's subjects to his modes, their mixture here suggests that, as the descriptive mode is becoming increasingly difficult to sustain, so too is the vision of Eden that is its subject. Clare's regard seems to be shifting in this poem, and in his poetry of the early 1830s as a whole, from victimized nature to the victimizer, and the shift is accompanied by a gradual change in predominant mode.

Until the early 1830s, Clare seems to have seen the fall from Eden as an event enacted mainly by others. He was, however, seriously affected economically and socially by the rural revolution; indeed his economic situation was such that by 1831 he owed two years' rent on his cottage in Helpston. When Lord Milton offered him the tenancy of another cottage in the neighboring village of Northborough, where he might set up as a smallholder, Clare accepted. In January 1832 he moved, but work was even harder to find than in Helpston, and by the spring of the following year Clare's debts from Helpston days had nearly doubled. More important, he had underestimated the effect on himself of the move from the place that had seen his greatest joy as well as his worst poverty.[28]

Before the move to Northborough, Clare regarded himself as largely unaffected spiritually and morally by enclosure; he saw no signs within himself of the cruelty and pride characteristic of fallen men, and he seems to have felt essentially apart from them. The vision of Edenic nature that required innocence was still intact for him. During the 1830s, however, the magnitude of the crime of enclosure seems to have convinced him of the inclusion of himself

---

28. The Tibbles describe Clare's reluctance to leave when the moment for departure came (*Life*, pp. 152, 147).

in its moral consequences, and the move to Northborough, which cut him off from his childhood nature, was conclusive. The move became his personal fall, a loss of the joy and enthusiasm of the Edenic vision. The poems that he wrote to describe this loss are the equivalent in Clare's canon of the odes of Wordsworth and Coleridge, "Intimations of Immortality," "Peele Castle," and "Dejection." Each work records a loss of vision and imagination, which in turn results in a loss of creative ability. Wordsworth in his achievement of maturity has lost his vision of "the splendour in the grass," and Coleridge, like Clare, has lost the experience of joy. Clare, however, finds no compensation in the wisdom or "humanised" soul of age as Wordsworth does; and, although his dejection is personal like Coleridge's, it is not solely that, for he is lamenting his own tragedy against the background of England's tragedy. Joy has passed from the people since they have lost their freedom and spontaneity, from the land since it has been subjected to the cruelty of man, and finally from himself because enclosure has prevented his vision of Eden and forced him through his ineradicable humanity to accept his fall and human isolation.

Northborough is only a few miles from Helpston, but for Clare the distance was unimportant and the change everything. Since it was not his childhood place, the new scene had the effect of an alien country on him, and the move was as deep and pervasive for him as the uprooting from their homes for the natural things in "Shadows of Taste": "Association fades and like a dream / They are but shadows of the things they seem" (SP, p. 116). In his letters of the period and in his dejection poems, Clare describes his move and loss of vision in terms of Adam's expulsion from Eden. In 1831, before his removal, Clare wrote to Taylor of enclosure's destruction of many of the natural things that had developed taste in him as a child.[29] His removal is a similar deprivation: "I have had some difficulties to leave the woods & heaths & favourite spots that have known me so long for the very molehills on the heath & the old trees in the hedges seem bidding me farewell . . . altho my flitting

---

29. *Letters*, p. 257. Men who enclose are often described as tasteless or with vulgar taste, a description that suggests enclosure as an extension of their fall to others. See "The Village Minstrel" (I, 156) and "The Mores" (*SP*, p. 169).

is not above three miles off—there is neither wood nor heath furze bush molehill or oak tree about it & a Nightingale never reaches as far in her summer excursions."[30]

There are several strands in Clare's three dejection poems; he is responding to the enclosure movement and to his own exile that somehow becomes an extension of it. The poems describe his loss of vision as a result of the severance of his links with childhood nature and also of man's sin of cruelty expressed in enclosure. They show the effect of man's corruption on his taste and perception of nature, and on the poetry that embodies them. In "Decay" (SP, p. 182), Clare is most concerned with man's estranged and un-Edenic view of nature.[31] He presents the fading of vision:

> The fields grow old and common things
> The grass the sky the winds a blowing
> And spots where still a beauty clings
> Are sighing 'going all a going' (SP, p. 182).

At first nature is described in the language of Clare's Edenic vision, but the refrain of poetry's decline suggests that the vision it records is declining. The result in the second part of the poem is a cold, inanimate world, all that is left to man without taste and true poetry. The sun now becomes a homeless ranger in the sky and the stream a common stream, and man can no longer respond with joy to natural things. So Eden for him passes from the world; once the "flowers upon the hills" had been "flowers from Adams open gardens," but the past tense gives way to the present:

> The sky hangs oer a broken dream
> The brambles dwindled to a bramble
> O poesy is on its wane
> I cannot find her haunts again (SP, p. 183).

---

30. *Letters*, p. 258. This letter was never sent to Taylor. The habit of writing but not sending letters increased as Clare's mental condition declined.

31. J. W. Tibble assigns this poem to the 1824–32 period when Clare was still at Helpston. Robinson and Summerfield claim it is from the Northborough years. Its subject matter certainly supports the latter assertion.

The immediate cause of the fall and loss is not stated in "Decay," but it is implied in the repetition of "naked," an adjective so often used in earlier poems for the ravaging effects of enclosure.[32]

The loss of taste attendant on the fall is treated again in "The Flitting" (SP, p. 176), where Clare presents not the debased vision of nature, which poetry's decline must indicate, but the degenerate poetry itself, which reflects man's new alienation from nature in its topics and their treatment. The new poets turn from nature to the exotic, a preference Clare had already berated in his essay on landscape painting. In "Shadows of Taste," he had asserted that true sublimity lies not in the huge and unusual, but in common nature. Here he states the proposition again:

> Some sing the pomps of chivalry
> As legends of the ancient time
> Where gold and pearls and mystery
> Are shadows painted for sublime
> But passions of sublimity
> Belong to plain and simpler things
> And David underneath a tree
> Sought when a shepherd Salems springs
>
> Where moss did unto cushions spring
> Forming a seat of velvet hue
> A small unnoticed trifling thing
> To all but heavens hailing dew
> And Davids crown hath passed away
> Yet poesy breaths his shepherd-skill
> His palace lost and to this day
> The little moss is blooming still (SP, p. 178).

As always, the sublimity of natural things comes from their Edenic qualities of eternity, beauty, and freedom; they are "coeval . . . with adams race" and the first to have seen God. Following this assertion of nature's worth, Clare presents his true poetry of common things:

---

32. See "The Lamentations of Round Oak Waters" (I, 70) and "The Lament of Swordy Well" (I, 420).

> I love the verse that mild and bland
> Breaths of green fields and open sky
> I love the muse that in her hand
> Bears wreaths of native poesy
> Who walks nor skips the pasture brook
> In scorn—but by the drinking horse
> Leans oer its little brig to look
> How far the sallows lean accross (*SP*, pp. 180–81).

But this poetic credo, the summary of so much Clare had written in the 1820s, is made at the moment when poetry can no longer be what he demands, for, when taste is gone, pride makes the muse "fear to stain her gown." It is the sad irony of this poem, as of the dejection odes of Wordsworth and Coleridge, that the poet successfully records his own joy in nature poetry, while asserting that it is no longer attainable: "Ive left my own old home of homes / Green fields and every pleasant place." In his new surroundings the summer comes "like a stranger" and the bird's song is "strange"; there is "no memory anywhere" and the harmony in which the poet and nature had lived in the old place where there were "green lanes that shut out burning skies / And old crooked stiles to rest upon" is broken. Yet Clare in "The Flitting" finds some consolation for his and all men's losses, that perhaps it is a loss of their joy only and not of nature's, for "still the grass eternal springs."

In the last of his dejection poems, "Remembrances" (*SP*, p. 174), there is no consolation in resilient nature, for the connections lacking in "Decay" and "The Flitting" are made here, and the total catastrophe, personal, public, and ecological, comes before the reader. "Remembrances" is one of Clare's most successful poems. It is written in a meter which John Hamilton Reynolds had used in his poem "On Revisiting Shrewsbury" and Clare had experimented with in "The Old Man's Lament" (II, 98), varying eight-, seven-, and six-beat lines. For his elegy on human joy and nature's Eden he chose an admirable stanza. The swelling movement of the first nine long lines is interrupted by the shortened last line, so that the stanzaic pattern parallels the matter of the poem, the surge of memories and the abrupt curtailing of them. The emphatic rhymes, both at the ends of lines and often in the middle, stress the finality of the loss; as the rhymes become inevitable and emphatic, so does the loss. The poem has the effect not of an outgush of despairing emotion but of a thoughtful summary of final despair, a litany rather than a lyric of grief.

The emphasized aspect of the fall in "Remembrances" is Clare's personal loss of his childhood. The meaning of this loss for him is expressed in a series of vignettes that convey the joys and raptures of childhood yet distance them through the presence of the older narrator:

> When jumping time away on old cross berry way
> And eating awes like sugar plumbs ere they had lost the may
> And skipping like a leveret before the peep of day
> On the rolly poly up and down of pleasant Swordy well
> When in round oaks narrow lane as the south got black again
> We sought the hollow ash that was shelter from the rain
> With our pockets full of pease we had stolen from the grain
> How delicious was the dinner time on such a showery day
> O words are poor reciepts for what time hath stole away
> The ancient pulpit trees and the play (*SP*, p. 174).

Not until Dylan Thomas' "Fern Hill" was childhood pleasure to be so evocatively described and lamented.

In *The Shepherd's Calendar*, Clare had seen the social decline of his rural society as a movement from summer to winter. In "Remembrances" his own fall is also expressed in terms of the seasonal change. Childhood's pleasures are "summers pleasures," and at the beginning of the poem the narrator is anticipating the decline of the year: "The cloudy days of autumn and of winter cometh on." The seasonal changes connect the several losses of the land and the narrator. The bareness of winter is the enclosed bareness of the land, for the tampering with nature has caused perpetual winter. The image of the flock of birds flying from the "naked spring" suggests the poet's boyhood pleasures departing and, in the process, draws attention to the "naked" land, despoiled not by seasonal winter but by enclosures. It becomes clear in the third stanza of the poem that the poet's childhood memories have been obliterated by the destruction of the nature of his youth. The "little mouldiwarps hang sweeing to the wind" where the molehills once were, and the places "where bramble bushes grew and the daisey gemmed in dew / And the hills of silken grass" are overlaid in his memory by the present reality:

> All leveled like a desert by the never weary plough
> All banished like the sun where that cloud is passing now
> And settled here for ever on its brow (*SP*, p. 175).

Irrevocable age, unmitigated by the memory of childhood joy, has come to the poet with the advent of perpetual winter.

By the end of the poem, the reality has conquered all memories, and the poet is forced to concentrate on the present benighted condition of himself and the land. The summer's decline into winter, foreshadowed in the first two lines, has been effected: winter has "come at last." Enclosure has triumphed and the coldness of the winter it brings has frozen summer joys and created a wasteland:

> ... I found the pleasure past and a winter come at last
> Then the fields were sudden bare and the sky got over cast
> And boy hoods pleasing haunts like a blossom in the blast
> Was shrivelled to a withered weed and trampled down and done
> Till vanished was the morning spring and set the summer sun
> And winter fought her battle strife and won (*SP*, p. 175).

The end of the poem returns to the poet's own loss, set now against the background of the universal fall. Here he accepts his own part in the decay, lamenting only that he did not "treasure up the may," the symbol of his past joy with nature. It is a symbol that emphasizes the impossibility of resisting the universal decline into winter.

"Remembrances" expresses the quintessence of Clare's belief in the fall. He has lost his faith, not primarily in nature's Eden as an ideal, but in man. The ideal, then, did not disintegrate under the weight of its own contradictions but was forcibly destroyed by society. The effect of its loss on Clare was deeper than his earlier loss of the social ideal, for, since nature was so intimately connected with poetry and taste, it was a loss of his own vision, a blow to his own poetic identity. The separation of man and nature Clare had seen at first only in the village people he now found in himself. For this personal alienation, there was no immediate resolution.

In Clare's philosophical nature poems of the 1820s, the theory of nature's Eden was asserted, while it remained implicit in the descriptive bird poems. In the 1830s the dejection poems assert Clare's belief in the fall of man, including himself, while a group of descriptive animal poems, written between 1835 and 1837, imply the resultant total separation of man from natural things. Thus the otherness that Clare had always stressed as a characteristic of nature becomes in these verses its dominant quality for man, and the world becomes the scene of the civil war Clare had been foretelling as early as "The Village Minstrel" (I, 155).

The overall shift in importance between the two poetic modes variously employed by Clare—the descriptive, and the lyrical and assertive—is momentarily halted in the animal poems. The tension of the breakdown of the descriptive mode revealed in "The Destroyer" is replaced in the animal poems by a tension of memory. The old golden descriptive poems comment on and darken the new wintry ones. This tension, added to the minute delineation of nature, always a feature of Clare's use of the descriptive mode, makes the animal poems as compelling and intense as the best of his assertive lyrics. Paradoxically, then, the descriptive mode reaches its most distinctive expression in the late poems of 1835 to 1837, poems which represent Clare's last major treatment of external nature for its own sake and his last major use of the descriptive mode.

In the poems before 1835, describing the destruction of Eden, Clare had conveyed the prelapsarian world through memories and contrasts, for his subject had been mainly the dramatic process of the fall. In the animal poems, however, Clare describes only the wintry world after the fall. He looks at the natural things, but neither identifies with them nor personifies them. Here, the georgic descriptive method of plain statement without intrusive emotional bias is used to convey a vision that is shocking; in addition, the economy, abruptness, and detail of the poems make it somehow impossible that their matter should be doubted.[33]

"The Badger," "The Marten," "The Hedgehog," and "The Fox"[34] are all similar in form; they are groups of sonnets that make up single poems. Throughout the pre-asylum years, the sonnet is one of Clare's most popular forms. In his earliest work, it is used largely for moral analogies drawn from nature; in the 1820s, however, it becomes on the whole descriptive.[35] A typical sonnet of this time presents precisely and particularly one or more visual images, rarely with any overt human significance or symbolic connotation. Soon, however, Clare seems to have found the form restrictive, and, in a letter of 1820, he scoffs at those who would make "readers believe a Sonnet cannot be a Sonnet unless it be precisly 14 lines."[36] To avoid the brevity of the descriptive sonnet, while keeping its particularity and conciseness, Clare evolved the sonnet group. Each sonnet can to some extent stand alone, but the connection between them remains closer than is usual in a sonnet sequence. In the animal sonnets of the 1830s there is sometimes an incipient narrative line that seems to require their continuous reading, but there is no conclusion in the final sonnet beyond the particulars presented, and each sonnet can be regarded as a whole descriptive incident.

The animals described in the sonnet groups are comparable in their lack of most of the usual Edenic qualities, although a certain bravery and secrecy remain to them. The poems show the invasion of this secrecy by man. "The Badger" (*SP*, p. 84) is a description of badger baiting, in which the animal is treated with extended human cruelty; the people "bait him all the day with many dogs."

33. Clare's animal poems resemble those of twentieth-century writers, "Fish" and "Humming-Bird" of D. H. Lawrence, for example.
34. Robinson and Summerfield enclose in square brackets the titles of the animal poems of this period.
35. Durling considers Clare's descriptive sonnets to be like "unassembled elements of a typical descriptive poem" (p. 186), and Robinson and Summerfield call them "pen-and-ink sketches of the great painter" (*SP*, p. xxviii).
36. *Letters*, p. 56.

THE LOSS OF EDEN

He fights fiercely and well, escaping from the crowd of his persecutors. But man's cruelty is persistent; the badger is chased with dogs and men until finally he is overcome:

> He turns agen and drives the noisey crowd
> And beats the many dogs in noises loud
> He drives away and beats them every one
> And then they loose them all and set them on
> He falls as dead and kicked by boys and men
> Then starts and grins and drives the crowd agen
> Till kicked and torn and beaten out he lies
> And leaves his hold and cackles groans and dies (SP, p. 86).

There is no explicit moral judgment in "The Badger," although it is implied in the description of the badger as "dimute and small," and in the presentation of man's savage joy in cruelty. In addition, no clear emotional bias emerges. Even during the badger's persecution and death there is no intrusive pity, for the verbs are unadorned and his death is robbed of our immediate sympathy by the unattractive word "cackles." Again, the energetic bravery of the badger is undercut by the last sonnet which describes a tamed badger who "licks the patting hand and tries to play / And never tries to bite or run away": nature is not only beaten, but humiliated.

In the endless civil war of the fallen world, man, the overall winner, is not always the conquerer in incidental battles. In "The Marten" (SP, p. 86), the hunters invade the animal's secrecy in a way Clare had warned against in his earlier poems. But here the owl wins the contest, and so leaves the marten free for the time being:

> When the grey owl her young ones cloathed in down
> Seizes the boldest boy and drives him down
> They try agen and pelt to start the fray
> The grey owl comes and drives them all away
> And leaves the martin twisting round his den
> Left free from boys and dogs and noise and men (SP, p. 87).

So too the fox (SP, p. 87), in spite of persistent persecution, "lived to chase the hounds another day." Yet man's defeat never mitigates his cruelty. The fox may win, but the human attitude toward him has already been fully expressed. The plowman

> ... found a weary fox and beat him out
> The ploughman laughed and would have ploughed him in
> But the old shepherd took him for the skin
> He lay upon the furrow stretched and dead
> The old dog lay and licked the wounds that bled
> The ploughman beat him till his ribs would crack
> And then the shepherd slung him at his back (*SP*, p. 87).

If the cruelty of man is pervasive in the poems, so too is nature's strangeness, almost repulsiveness, for man. These qualities are best conveyed in "The Hedgehog" (*SP*, p. 88); the hedgehog is initially repulsive, but by the end of the poem he wins a kind of grudging sympathy from the reader. During the first description, the hedgehog is referred to as "he," a designation that remains until Clare portrays man's hunting of him. Then "he" becomes "it," a referential method that reflects the human attitude toward the hedgehog, who changes from a little animal filling a nest and hunting for crabs and sloes to "black and bitter and unsavoury meat." The gypsies are the only people who eat the hedgehog meat, and they have something of the animal's strangeness, living on the periphery of humanity. But their position there allows them a better understanding of the hedgehog then the hunters have. They have seen his vulnerability and gentleness, while those who find the meat distasteful and despise the gypsies see the hedgehog only as a victim for their cruelty:

> But they who hunt the field for rotten meat
> And wash in muddy dyke and call it sweat [*sic*]
> And eat what dogs refuse where ere they dwell
> Care little either for the taste or smell
> They say they milk the cows and when they lye
> Nibble their fleshy teats and make them dry
> But they whove seen the small head like a hog
> Rolled up to meet the savage of a dog

With mouth scarce big enough to hold a straw
Will neer believe what no one ever saw
But still they hunt the hedges all about
And shepherd dogs are trained to hunt them out
They hurl with savage force the stick and stone
And no one cares and still the strife goes on (*SP,* pp. 88–89).

The image of vulnerability and gentleness seen only by the gypsies is a typical example of the effect of Clare's animal poems of this time. The image is unpleasant and alien at first; yet by the side of man's familiar ferocity, it becomes, while remaining strange, a positive expression of the hedgehog's tender quality. This strange tenderness and vulnerability of natural things that are grotesque and unpleasant to human sight exactly express the new situation for Clare.[37] Nature might retain some of its Edenic qualities, but for man they are now veiled.

Man's imperception is implied in the animal poems by the grotesque and alien appearance of nature to him. This appearance is minutely described but not explicitly judged or condemned. Yet, although the "emotional and philosophical appearance" of poetry which Taylor required is absent, as it has been from all Clare's predominantly descriptive verse, the images presented in "The Badger" and "The Hedgehog" disturb the reader into his own emotion and thought. With the combination of descriptive visual power and the power to disturb, the animal sonnets represent the summit of Clare's long experimentation with the georgic descriptive mode.

The animal poems represent, too, a symbolic summation, the final act in the dramatic loss of human perception. By 1837 Clare's treatment of the fall from Eden had apparently been worked out. The enclosure movement, posing at first a threat to the pleasant rural society of his youth, became a greater menace to the land, an object more vulnerable and valuable than the decaying human society. Because of the connection of his ideal with reality, and because of the nature of his descriptive mode, Clare's belief in Eden

37. In "The Mouse's Nest" (II, 370), the narrator is repulsed by the mouse and her young so that he feels nature alien. Yet the animal's tenderness and careful secrecy are somehow conveyed around him without mitigation of the strangeness.

could not withstand the destruction of the pure natural things that had held Eden within themselves and had connected him with his childhood joy. Simultaneously, the enclosure movement assaulted his belief by suggesting a human depravity so total that not even an isolated poet could escape it. The resultant un-Edenic vision is frightening in its stark truthfulness and in the extent of the loss it implies.

It is useless to speculate on the causes of the madness that overtook Clare in 1837 and confined him to an asylum for most of the remainder of his life. It may have been hereditary, or the result of poverty and suffering as Dr. Allen of his first asylum implied.[38] Perhaps again, like Ruskin, Clare might have said, "I went mad because nothing came of my work."[39] Whatever its cause, Clare's approaching insanity can be seen in his animal poems of the later 1830s, not in any confusion or contradiction, but in the disturbing quality of the vision and in the despair that is its background. It is also perhaps reflected in his symbolic pattern of Eden and the fall. The external Edenic world had been a satisfying ideal for him and its minute delineation had been the poet's proper occupation. His fellows, however, had apparently extended their fallen condition to him, and consequently Edenic nature had been hidden from him. After 1837, although Clare achieves a modified and desultory belief in his own Edenic nature vision, he never again sees this Eden clearly or exhibits wholly that taste which had once seen the "dayshine" on the world.

38. *Life,* pp. 173, 163.
39. John Ruskin, "Letter 88," *Fors Clavigera,* in *The Works of John Ruskin,* eds. E. T. Cook and Alexander Wedderburn (London: George Allen, 1903–12), 29:386.

5
The Creative Eden

CLARE'S symbolic pattern of Eden and the fall, expressed in his poetry, is a traditional one, adumbrated in the Christian myth of the fall, and, nearer to Clare's time, in the works of Thomson and Blake. The interpretation of this pattern is, however, unique to Clare and is contingent on the elements of his life and times and on the results of his own philosophical exploration. The golden age he described in his early poetry reflected the Helpston of his childhood and of his early maturity, and the Edenic nature was the nature which nurtured his own taste and was in turn illuminated by it. When his perception of a golden age and of Edenic nature failed, he turned to the expression of sorrow at its passing and to an exploration of the human perceptual failure.

Enclosure, the symptom and cause of the fall, is, even in the early poems, most felt in its effect on man's perception. Yet it represents also the encroachment of man onto nature and of the most corrupted men onto the least, the peasants who tilled enough land only for their own need and expressed their nearness to and respect for nature in their country rites. Clare responded to enclosure in a dual way: as a poet who had lost his ideal and as a peasant whose way of life had been shattered.

Clare's conceptions of poetry, taste, and God are developed rather than changed as his various ideals fade. His belief in the golden age and Eden perhaps necessitated a conception of poetry as imitation, for he described Eden when he described the external world. The function of poetry for him is in accordance with this imitative conception: to lead men at first toward an appreciation of a passing society, later toward an awareness of the innocence and otherness of external nature, and finally toward a realization of all men's perceptual loss.

Clare's conception of taste is contingent on his conception of poetry and the poet. Taste is a distinguishing faculty; it allows Edenic perception in the world and it bestows the ability to reproduce this in verbal images. Its fading is, therefore, a loss of actual vision and of poetic ability.

Throughout Clare's work, God remains a transcendent deity. In the pre-asylum poems, He seems a fairly distant Creator, although he bestows His "image" on natural things. Nature's presence is more felt than its Maker's, and nature's earthly beauty is stressed over God's divine beauty. This is perhaps in keeping with Clare's emphasis on the unknowability of God and on the presumption and stupidity of limited men who seek to measure Him. Clare's attitude of humility is expressed constantly in his distrust of prideful science and in his dislike of religious sects purporting to know God's mind.

Of the institutional church and its doctrines, Clare remains usually skeptical. He vacillates in his belief in a compensatory afterlife, but, on the whole, he seems to have denied it, just as he usually denies any soteriological system. Men fell by their own wills and pride rather than through original sin, and there is no suggestion that they can rise again, except through understanding and somehow attaining the innocence of the nature they are destroying. The negative and skeptical attitude Clare reveals toward institutional and doctrinal religion contrasts with his positive and deferential attitude to the unknowable God. But both perhaps spring from the same source: his belief in man's limitation and achieved depravity.

A study of Clare's quest for the Edenic ideal and of its contingent topics necessarily entails his comparison with the major Romantics. It is perhaps a measure of his greatness that he is not diminished by this comparison, which reveals his commonality with them and his distinction. This commonality and distinction make his poetic thought a necessary addition and qualification to the poetic thought of his age. In his poetry Clare merges the reverence for the autonomy of the nonhuman, characteristic of the georgic descriptive poets, with the deep poetic commitment and idealist concern of his contemporaries, to form a blend of descriptive idealism that is unique in his age. His social significance is also unique. As a peasant he recorded the ecological and economic changes felt most nearly by his peers, and yet he subordinated their tragedy to the moral and spiritual tragedy that he felt was befalling the land and all its inhabitants.

An assessment of Clare's work can be based partly on its philosophical and social importance. In 1832, however, Clare wrote of the volume later to be called *The Rural Muse*, "I wish to be judged of by the book itself without any appeals to want of education lowness of origin or any other foil that officion [officiousness?] chuses to encumber my path with."[1] The assessment of Clare's work needs, therefore, to rest finally on poetic merit. Robert Graves has said of Clare that, in contrast to Wordsworth, he "began as a servant of the public, but ended as a devotee of the Goddess."[2] It is doubtful that Clare was ever truly a servant of the public, however much he desired the rewards accruing from such a position, but in the mid-1820s there certainly appears in his work a stronger commitment than before to poetry, to the exploration of its purpose and to the perfection of its craft. The result was that at his best he attained to that excellence which, in his own words, "must be its own creation."

1. *Letters*, p. 267.
2. *The Crowning Privilege* (1955; New York: Doubleday, 1956), p. 56.

UNIVERSITY OF FLORIDA MONOGRAPHS

Humanities

No. 1: *Uncollected Letters of James Gates Percival*, edited by Harry R. Warfel

No. 2: *Leigh Hunt's Autobiography: The Earliest Sketches*, edited by Stephen F. Fogle

No. 3: *Pause Patterns in Elizabethan and Jacobean Drama*, by Ants Oras

No. 4: *Rhetoric and American Poetry of the Early National Period*, by Gordon E. Bigelow

No. 5: *The Background of* The Princess Casamassima, by W. H. Tilley

No. 6: *Indian Sculpture in the John and Mable Ringling Museum of Art*, by Roy C. Craven, Jr.

No. 7: *The Cestus. A Mask*, edited by Thomas B. Stroup

No. 8: *Tamburlaine, Part I, and Its Audience*, by Frank B. Fieler

No. 9: *The Case of John Darrell: Minister and Exorcist*, by Corinne Holt Rickert

No. 10: *Reflections of the Civil War in Southern Humor*, by Wade H. Hall

No. 11: *Charles Dodgson, Semeiotician*, by Daniel F. Kirk

No. 12: *Three Middle English Religious Poems*, edited by R. H. Bowers

No. 13: *The Existentialism of Miguel de Unamuno*, by José Huertas-Jourda

No. 14: *Four Spiritual Crises in Mid-Century American Fiction*, by Robert Detweiler

No. 15: *Style and Society in German Literary Expressionism*, by Egbert Krispyn

No. 16: *The Reach of Art: A Study in the Prosody of Pope*, by Jacob H. Adler

No. 17: *Malraux, Sartre, and Aragon as Political Novelists*, by Catharine Savage

No. 18: *Las Guerras Carlistas y el Reinado Isabelino en la Obra de Ramón del Valle-Inclán*, por María Dolores Lado

No. 19: *Diderot's* Vie de Sénèque: *A Swan Song Revised*, by Douglas A. Bonneville

No. 20: *Blank Verse and Chronology in Milton*, by Ants Oras

No. 21: *Milton's Elisions*, by Robert O. Evans

No. 22: *Prayer in Sixteenth-Century England*, by Faye L. Kelly

No. 23: *The Strangers: The Tragic World of Tristan L'Hermite*, by Claude K. Abraham

No. 24: *Dramatic Uses of Biblical Allusion in Marlowe and Shakespeare*, by James H. Sims

No. 25: *Doubt and Dogma in Maria Edgeworth*, by Mark D. Hawthorne

No. 26: *The Masses of Francesco Soriano*, by S. Philip Kniseley

No. 27: *Love as Death in* The Iceman Cometh, by Winifred Dusenbury Frazer

No. 28: *Melville and Authority*, by Nicholas Canaday, Jr.

No. 29: *Don Quixote: Hero or Fool? A Study in Narrative Technique*, by John J. Allen

No. 30: *Ideal and Reality in the Fictional Narratives of Théophile Gautier*, by Albert B. Smith

No. 31: *Negritude as a Theme in the Poetry of the Portuguese-Speaking World*, by Richard A. Preto-Rodas

No. 32: *The Criticism of Photography as Art: The Photographs of Jerry Uelsmann*, by John L. Ward

No. 33: *The Kingdom of God in the Synoptic Tradition*, by Richard H. Hiers

No. 34: *Dante Gabriel Rossetti's Versecraft*, by Joseph F. Vogel

No. 35: *T. S. Eliot's Concept of Language: A Study of Its Development*, by Harry T. Antrim

No. 36: *The Consolatio Genre in Medieval English Literature*, by Michael H. Means

No. 37: *Melville's Angles of Vision*, by A. Carl Bredahl, Jr.

No. 38: *The Historical Jesus and the Kingdom of God*, by Richard H. Hiers

No. 39: *In Adam's Garden: A Study of John Clare's Pre-Asylum Poetry*, by Janet M. Todd